The Transcendent Child

The Transcendent Child

Tales of Triumph
Over the Past

LILLIAN B. RUBIN

BasicBooks
A Division of HarperCollins*Publishers*

Designed by Elliott Beard

Library of Congress Cataloging-in-Publication Data
Rubin, Lillian B.
      The transcendent child : tales of triumph over the
past / Lillian B. Rubin.
          p.   cm.
      ISBN 0-465-08669-1
      1. Problem families—United States—Case studies.   2. Adult
children of dysfunctional families—United States—Case studies.
      I. Title.
HQ536.R76   1996
362.82—dc20   95-24895
                                                                  CIP

96 97 98 99 ❖/RRD 9 8 7 6 5 4 3 2 1

Contents

Acknowledgments

No book is ever the product of a single person. From the time an idea is first spoken until the last word is written, there are others who stand in the background, yet who make their mark. For their part in this background drama, I want to thank Troy Duster, Sam Gerson, Dorothy Jones, Michael Kimmel, and Joyce Lipkis, whose critical readings of all or part of the manuscript were enormously helpful.

Four friends—Kim Chernin, Diane Ehrensaft, Ruth Goldman, and Michael Rogin—were so intimately involved from beginning to end that they were more foreground than background. Words of thanks on a page can hardly do justice to their contribution, not just to this book but to my life and well-being. Theirs are friendships of extraordinary durability that, even after many years, continue to offer the special combination of intellectual companionship and emotional support we all dream of finding.

It has been a great gift to work with Steve Fraser, my editor. His ability to grasp the meaning of the work I was trying to do even when it was not yet fully formed, his splendid editorial eye, and his invariably intelligent responses have been invaluable.

Rhoda Weyr, my agent, rates an A-plus for both her critical reading and her many years of unfailing support.

My deepest love and gratitude go to my husband, Hank Rubin; my daughter, Marci Rubin; and her partner, Larry Harrigan, who provided the background of loving support every writer needs. Hank not only read every word of every draft but was a sounding board for every idea in this book. Marci's reading was, as always, intelligent and perceptive. And Larry was always there to make me laugh. Without their love, friendship, and intellectual nourishment, my life and my work would be measurably poorer.

Finally, there are the women and men whose stories I tell on these pages. They are the most important contributors of all, for without them, there would be no book. I shall always be indebted to them for allowing me into their lives—a debt I can repay only by honoring not just the content of their stories but the spirit of their lives. More than anything else, I have tried to do that. It is to them—Sara Mikoulis, Petar Steprovic, Lynne Halsted, Wayne Morgan, Ana Guttierez, Kevin McLaren, Karen Richards, and Chris Lydon—that I dedicate this book with my heartfelt gratitude.

one

Fall Down Seven Times, Get Up Eight

AS A CHILD RAISED IN A FAMILY WHERE DEATH, POVERTY, DEPRESSION, and a mother's nearly psychotic rage determined daily life, I have lived with both the guilt and the wonder of being the transcendent child, the one who overcame the deficits of that past when my brother could not. *Why me and not him?* I asked myself a thousand times as I watched his painful—and often failed—struggle to manage his life successfully.

Then not long ago, he was killed in an automobile accident that looked more like a suicide. Any death is cause for remembering, for reflection. But the circumstances of my brother's death, his carelessness with his own life, if not his willful shutting it off, raised for me more sharply than ever before the question: Why did he get stuck in our frightful past? How did I escape?

Why me? It's a question that haunts every transcendent child, a question we ask painfully, guiltily—and also triumphantly. In his book *Brothers and Keepers,* John Edgar Wideman, struggling to understand why he is a successful writer and professor of English while his brother is serving a life sentence for murder, recalls his mother talking about how Robby was different, how he was looking for excitement from the day he was born. Bad seed? Wideman asks.

Certainly, the tangled strands of DNA that determine our genetic predispositions make a difference in how we respond to the world around us. In my own family, my brother's pessimism and my optimism stood in opposition to one another from our earliest childhood. He characteristically saw a half empty glass; to my eyes, it was always half full. Such differences are not trivial. They govern how we experience the world, how we internalize and interact with those experiences, what choices seem possible.

But the secrets and possibilities embedded in the double helix notwithstanding, it alone cannot explain why some people fall down seven times and get up eight—and why others cannot recover from the first fall. For although the process by which we respond to events around us may be influenced by our genes, it is mediated by the social and psychological circumstances within which our lives are embedded.

In twenty-five years as a practicing psychotherapist, I have often found myself awed by the ability of some people to transcend their hurtful past and, against all odds, find pathways to a satisfying adulthood. Yet virtually every twentieth-century theory on which clinical psychology rests, from psychoanalysis to behaviorism, insists that the earliest experience of a child's life *in the family* foretells the rest.

Even casual observation suggests, however, that it's not possible to write a biography before a life has been lived. Certainly, the past counts. A good start—a parent who provides what D. W. Winnicott calls a "holding environment" in the first years of life, for example—can make a difference in a person's capacity to form attachments later on. Similarly, a bad start—abuse, abandonment, neglect in early life—take their toll.

But the idea that what happens to a child in those early years in the family *determines* the future is much too simple. It assumes, first, that the child is a passive receptacle; second, that the experiences of early childhood inevitably dwarf everything that happens afterward. In reality, however, how the child *handles* those early experiences makes a difference in the outcome. As does what happens in the years ahead.

True, as the stories that follow show, the characteristics that allow a child to transcend a difficult past are evident early on. But too much intervenes between infancy and adulthood for the experience in the family alone to govern how a life will be lived. Particular psychological proclivities, class background, subcultural differences, personal experiences, and the way they are internalized all play a part in the making of an adult—an idea that, once expressed, we intuitively recognize as true, yet one that has been neglected by both mental health practitioners and popular culture.

Developmental psychologists, on the other hand, have demonstrated a more complex view in recent years and are more likely to see human development as an ongoing process that is not subject to the kind of determinism that marks clinical theory. But the central debate among these theorists—whether there's continuity or discontinuity across the life span—is itself a problem. For when one looks at lives in process, it seems evident that there are both continuities and discontinuities, and that the kind of research we do, the way we focus the questions, will reveal one side or the other. Turn the prism one way, and we'll see discontinuity; look at it from the other side, and continuity comes into view.

This book is about women and men who have violated the psychological predictions and have transcended harsh and painful pasts. By *transcendence,* I don't mean that they have undergone some kind of psychological transformation in the years between childhood and adulthood. There are no miraculous rebirths here, no otherworldly revelations, no clean slate upon which a new life is cast. Rather, their adult lives are forged directly out of the past—a past whose torments and wounds have left scars that sometimes make themselves felt in the present. But the same strength and determination that got them through the trials of childhood enabled them also to find their way to satisfying adulthoods. Not perfect lives, to be sure, but highly functional ones in which, along with the problems of living, they have also known a fair share of joy and pleasure.

The central question of this work is: What makes such transcendence possible? Since existing theory offers few answers, I turned to people whose lives and experiences could teach us something new about the process of constructing a life. The stories on the pages that follow are taken from intimately detailed life-history interviews with men and women who fit the profile of the transcendent child. In them we can see some of the elements in the drama of human development that have long been neglected both by psychology's persistent focus on pathology and by its insistence on the singular importance of the "good family" in the developmental outcome.

Obviously, a good family is not irrelevant to a child's development. But the very fact that so many mental health professionals are thriving is testimony to how hard it is to come by. Nevertheless, we continue to write volumes about the impact of the family, both negative and positive, and about the centrality of, in D. W. Winnicott's well-worn phrase, the "good enough mother," as if these were the only influences in a child's life.

As these stories show, however, the abused child doesn't necessarily become a child abuser; the unloved child isn't destined to be unlovable; success and happiness in adulthood may not await the welcomed and adored child. Who hasn't known people whose childhoods seemed ideal, yet who grew up to become troubled adults? Who hasn't known others who have transcended early experiences that should have led to disaster? Who hasn't known alcoholic families in which one sibling drinks only moderately, if at all, and the others descend into the chaos that alcoholism breeds?

The question then is: What are the personal qualities and social conditions that make it possible for some people to flourish when they have grown up in "bad" families?

One major theme that emerges from these life histories is clear: *Some families have to be left behind.* And the transcendent child is one who, for a variety of reasons, is able to do that relatively early in life. But what does it mean to leave the family behind as a child?

At the most fundamental level, people who have transcended their pasts were very young when they first experienced themselves as marginal in the family. These were children who somehow didn't fit, children who were in the family but not of it and who, therefore, became the observers of family life. "I felt like a dog in the middle of a cat family, always on the outside watching," says Kevin McLaren.*

Such children tend to distance themselves very early, often as young as five or six. I am not speaking here of the ordinary separation struggle that all children must engage as they grow to maturity. Rather, the transcendent child actively leaves the family behind by *dis*identifying with it and its way of life.

In my own case, by the time I was five years old, my mother and I were already at war—a war in which each battle was not just a child's rebellion but another step in the process of disidentification. Then it was about food—vegetables, in particular. They were a Monday and Thursday night ritual at our house, partly because, my mother kept insisting, they were good for us, but mostly because we were poor and a "vegetable plate"—as this concoction of a baked potato stuffed with spinach, some overcooked carrots, and gray canned peas was known in the family—was cheap.

Patience was never my mother's long suit, a quality that has been passed through three generations of women in my family—from her to me to my daughter. At the first sign of my resistance, therefore, she'd stand over me, fork at the ready, and shout, "Open your mouth!" When my lips remained clamped shut, she'd grab my jaw with thumb and middle finger, pressing hard until the pain forced

---

*All names and identifying details have been changed, except where the material is a central feature of the narrative.

me to open my mouth. Then she'd shove the food in and hold my nose until I either choked or swallowed. When the plate was empty, she'd turn away with a satisfied, "There, that'll teach you."

But what it taught me was unclear. I soon learned to vomit when I wanted to, and after each such session I simply vomited up the food, sometimes all over the table.

My brother, who hated those vegetables as much as I did, choked them down silently as he watched the fireworks at the other side of the table. "Why don't you just eat them?" he'd ask me later. "I don't like them," was all I could say then. Years later I'd wonder about the difference between my brother's response to my mother's rageful authoritarianism and mine; wonder, too, what his passivity cost and what my stubborn determination wrought.

The advancing years did little to smooth my relationship with my mother. I like to think it was easier when my father, who died a few months after my fifth birthday, was still alive. But I don't know if that's true, since I have almost no memory of those earlier years. What I do know is that at age twenty-seven my mother, an illiterate immigrant who barely spoke English, was left alone in a strange land with two small children to support.

I can feel sympathy for that young woman today—sympathy and admiration for the courage and determination it took to pick up the pieces and make a life for her small family. But she was also cruel, especially to a daughter who seemed to her to be a reminder of the trials of womanhood. "Girls shouldn't be born," she'd say in a voice that, to my child's ears, sounded filled with scorn and hatred.

I was seven years old when, bewildered by her rage and hurt by her rejection, I began consciously to remove myself psychologically from the family scene. It was then that I first said to myself clearly, *I won't be like her.* This doesn't mean that I didn't need my mother, that I didn't long for her approval, that I didn't live in terror that she'd die and leave us as my father did, or even that I didn't love her as a child loves a parent. But in whatever way a seven-year-old knows, I also knew I didn't want to model myself on this person who was so angry and often so mean.

My renunciation notwithstanding, I was also my mother's daughter. Or as she would say in those rare moments when I succeeded in pleasing her (usually when she was showing off my report card), "The apple doesn't fall far from the tree." Words that angered me, even as her approval warmed me, because they seemed to take from me my accomplishment and to mean that, despite my efforts, I really was like her.

That was true in some ways, of course, not least in the kind of determination I was capable of when I made up my mind to do something. So when, at eight, a friend who had watched me walk down the street said as I approached, "You walk just like your mother," I spent the next year training myself to walk differently. To this day I monitor my walk from time to time, experiencing the same satisfaction I knew then when I no longer walked like her.

Outwardly I remained part of the family. I lived in the house, did what was expected, tried earnestly from time to time to relate to my brother, to please my mother—rarely with any success. When, in later years, she would occasionally speak of my childhood, my mother would acknowledge that I "never gave her any trouble," which meant she didn't have to worry about my grades in school or about my getting into scrapes on the street. But she'd also follow this somewhat grudging concession by complaining, "You were always peculiar, not like your brother."

It's certainly true that I was the child who didn't fit, the one who lived at the psychological margins of the family. For most of my childhood poverty forced us to live jammed together in a single room that left no private space, not even a bed of my own. Even in adolescence, when things eased a bit and we could afford a one-bedroom apartment, I still slept in the same bed with my mother while my brother had the living room couch. Yet many years later, when I took a course in family therapy and was asked to make a living sculpture of my

family, I placed the representations of my mother and brother together while the figure that was me stood off at some distance and
watched them warily.

It was a wrenching reminder of the aching, gripping loneliness of
my childhood, my conviction that I must be an adopted child to feel
so alien, my despairing fantasy that in some heroic, romantic quest I
would find my "true" family, the one in which I would finally belong.
None of that happened, of course, because this *was* my true family,
the family of my birth. A reality that left me with the choice—
although not consciously understood and articulated at the time—
between accepting my marginality and searching for comfort elsewhere, or trying to belong and getting stuck in the past. I chose
marginality, my brother belonging—a choice that freed me and left
him victimized by the web of pain, poverty, depression, and anger that
characterized the ethos of that family.

Sometimes it's the child who marginalizes himself by withdrawing
in alienation. Then family members, feeling hurt, angry, and uncomprehending, respond in kind, helping to entrench the pattern of
marginalization. Sometimes it's family members who initiate the
process by their collective inability to understand and cope with the
child who doesn't fit. Such a child often seems like an accusation to
the others, an unfriendly and judgmental observer in their midst.
Then the child reacts.

However it starts, it soon becomes a reciprocal system that circles
around and feeds upon itself, leaving the child increasingly isolated.
All too often children who find themselves in this situation spend
their lives knocking on a door that's closed to them. But those who
transcend their pasts soon become adept at finding and engaging
alternative sources of support. Almost always a surrogate, a mentor, a
model, a friend plays an important role in the life of the child—
assuaging the loneliness, presenting the possibility of another life, of
a different way of being.

Sometimes it's a real person—a teacher, a relative, a neighbor, a friend; sometimes one who lives in imagination alone—a stuffed animal that's anthropomorphized, a fantasy playmate, or an imaginary "good" parent to whom the child turns for comfort and consolation. In my own childhood, I invented a family, complete with a father, a loving stay-at-home mom who cooked cereal without lumps, a sister who was my emotional twin, a big brother who liked to play with me, and, not least, a bed of my own.

In real life, the more the transcendent child feels detached from the center of family life, the more she becomes involved in some arena of living that's far removed from family pursuits. One child buries herself in books in a household where no one reads. "I spent a lot of time taking the bus to the library," recalls Sara Mikoulis. "That was my pattern; it still is. I find something to throw myself into that keeps me engaged in something besides my own worries."

Another studies music despite the taunts of those around him. "They couldn't figure out what I was about," says Kevin McLaren. "They wanted me to be like everybody else, go outside, play with the other kids, be interested in sports. All I wanted to do was make music."

A third turns to religion in a family where this is inconsequential. "Going to church was like finding a room of my own, the first place where I felt at home, where I could hear myself and listen to my own inner life, and where I didn't feel unwelcome or threatened," explains Lynne Halsted. "There was a kind of calm there that I knew nothing about in my family."

Although such activities usually isolate the children still further, the ability to escape into them also contributes to a heightened sense of efficacy and a more autonomous sense of self. Whatever the outcome of the choices they make, it's the sense of marginality in the family, the feeling that they don't fit, that lays the psychological groundwork enabling them to see and grasp alternatives.

Psychological explanations, however, are not enough to explain the capacity to reach for opportunities. True, some people don't see options even when they're available. But it's one of the great failings of psychological theory that it doesn't adequately take account of the impact of the larger social milieu—whether economic, cultural, or political—on human development.

Certainly, as Robert Louis Stevenson once said, life isn't just a matter of holding good cards but of playing the bad ones well. But it's equally certain that the psychological resources we bring to the table can't be disentangled from the larger social context within which the hand must be played out. A poor child has fewer options and greater obstacles to overcome than a middle-class one. In a society where race often determines life chances, a child born into an African American, Latino, or Native American family has even more to surmount. The immigrant child who confronts an alien culture and a language she can't speak has a more difficult time than an American-born one. Women still are more handicapped than men in their attempts to develop lives that include both love and work.

Just as the social context of life can impede development, it can also facilitate it. Look, for example, at how feminism has made possible choices for women that were largely unavailable before, at how it has helped not just to change the rules and roles by which they live but the very identity they call their own. Or at the influence of the civil rights movement on both the identity of African Americans and the economy of that community.

It's true, as every therapist knows, that people whose lives are beset by pain and trauma often are so focused on themselves that they barely notice the world around them. Sara Mikoulis, for example, a black woman who suffered an excruciatingly brutal childhood, explains, "I know it's hard to understand, but I never thought about myself or anything that ever happened to me as connected to my race. I was so abused by my family, I thought it was my destiny. It was like everything fell into the same pot, so if someone said or did something to me because of my race, I wouldn't have noticed. It just seemed natural that I'd be abused by them, too." Nevertheless, whether consciously understood or not, the shifts and changes in the social world form the background of our lives and times, often opening options that were unavailable to earlier generations, allowing us to see what had been invisible before.

The women and men in this book come from a variety of backgrounds and from families that range from difficult to malignant. Their social, economic, and ethnic diversity made for childhood experiences that were sometimes so distant from one another that they might as well have lived in different universes. Ana Guttierez was the child of poverty who grew up in the shacks migrant farmworkers call home, while Lynne Halsted's family owned a half dozen homes in various cities around the globe and had a staff of sixty to attend to their needs wherever they happened to land. The tie that binds them is that each has transcended a difficult and painful past, usually in a way that their siblings have not.

They have, of course, also been molded by that past. But the form of the mold defies the expert predictions. The battered child is now a gentle and loving mother who sees it as her mission to spend part of her professional life working with abused children and their parents. The child who was the family isolate, whose early years show little evidence of any particular talent for social relatedness, grows up to be what I call here *adoptable*.

By adoptable, I mean the ability to attract others who, at various times in a life, become the mentors and surrogates who light the way and fill the gaps left by the past. It's a gift that's common among those who transcend their past—a gift that makes it easier to bear their travail, easier, too, to get up and move on each time they fall down.

Sometimes these are long-lasting relationships; often they are not. It makes no difference. Their importance lies in their *meaning* to the persons involved and in the fact that there is someone to hold out a hand in time of need, someone also who can help fill the empty spaces inside.

Just drawing such people in is not enough, however. As a therapist, I have seen many adults who might qualify for adoptability but who are too frightened to risk a trusting engagement with another. For an adoption to work, therefore, a person needs to know how to accept and use what others offer, which means, among other things, being open to a relationship and willing to risk enough to give oneself over to it.

A sense of mission—a commitment to something larger than self and personal interest—is prominent in most of the stories that follow as well. At the most obvious level, such a mission provides purpose and meaning in people's lives. For the men and women whose stories I tell here, the mission is related also to the gratitude they feel for having escaped their childhood sufferings—gratitude that expresses itself in a sense of indebtedness that impels them to try to pay back what they call their "good fortune."

In adulthood, therefore, they're not content just to revel in lives that are so different from what they knew in childhood. Instead, they want to use the experiences of the past to change the present, not just for themselves but for others as well. In doing so, they not only give meaning to their suffering but help to heal themselves.

The past, of course, leaves scars that, when picked, can bleed. But the transcendent child long ago learned to live with the pain. In fact, it often seems like a familiar if difficult friend who, for all the anguish, has played a positive role in the development of a life. The tolerance for pain—the ability to recognize it, to live with it, to accept it, to understand its source, and to master it—breeds the strength necessary for transcendence.

Each chapter in this book presents the life history of a person. Each story shows the person's place in the family, the choices and adaptations each made along the way to adulthood, and the social and psychological forces that made those choices possible. All together these narratives form a collage—a series of portraits of people whose characteristics and adaptations have enabled them to fall down seven times and get up eight.

As with all personal narratives, each story is a construction that reflects the individual's *experience* of his or her life. This doesn't mean it's a fiction. Rather, as Erik Erikson wrote in *Insight and Responsibility*, in every life story there are both the "actuality" and the "reality"—the former concerned with objective facts, the latter with how the individual *feels* about those facts. Certainly, facts count. But it's how those facts are experienced and remembered, how they're interpreted, what meaning is assigned to them, that's central not just in constructing the narrative of a life but in how that life actually is lived.

The process of remembering is itself a delicate one, guided in great part by the need to maintain an integrated and coherent sense of self. But *what* we remember and *how* we remember it may be more important than the event itself. Some people nurse and cradle memories of adversity as if they were gold, offering them up at every opportunity as explanations for their damaged lives. These are the men and women for whom the past lives as powerfully today as it did yesterday, who relate to the old hurts with the same sense of injury and helplessness they experienced as children.

Others repress and deny their painful past in the vain belief that if they close their eyes, it will cease to exist. But the cost of forgetting is high. To forget, we must dissociate ourselves from our history, silence thought, strip words from consciousness, armor the heart, smother the soul. Forgetting, then, is a symbolic death, obliterating not just what once was but who we are now and how we came to be that way.

The men and women on the pages of this book remember. They remember the pain and feel the sorrow, just as they did when they were children. But now as then, they're not rendered helpless by their experience. Instead, their lives are organized around transcending it, and their memories serve as a goad in the struggle to overcome. Their suffering is evident in the stories they tell. And so is their pride—pride in their stubborn refusal to succumb to even the bleakest environment; pride in having gotten up each time they fell, or more likely were pushed, down; pride in having foiled the predictors and beaten the odds.

The details of their childhood miseries may differ, but the common ground—then as now—on which they all stand is their dogged refusal to define themselves as victims, no matter how crushing their burdens. In a society where people clutch their victimhood to their breast like a badge of honor, where there are support groups for every kind of complaint, listening to the people whose lives are chronicled on these pages was, for me, like a breath of fresh air.

I don't mean to suggest that there are no legitimate grievances in our society or that support groups offer nothing but the opportunity for whining. But when our therapeutic culture meets the culture of complaint that surrounds us today, the same group that offers support often also facilitates, if it does not actually encourage, a continuing sense of victimhood.

On a trip to the Midwest a few months ago, for example, I saw a sign advertising a support group for "wounded daughters of distant fathers," and I didn't know whether to laugh or cry. What does it mean for a woman to think of herself as wounded? Why would anyone want to define herself that way? However a person answers these questions, such groups too often thrive on soliciting pain, encouraging people to fan it, to hold it tight, rather than helping them to heal.

Undoubtedly, it's useful for adult children of alcoholic parents to meet others who have suffered the same experience. But the group itself can also promote a kind of fatalistic resignation that becomes an excuse for not dealing with the problems of living that aren't much different from those we all encounter.

Similarly, the support groups that help men and women cope with the issues divorce raises may nurse a sense of victimhood that impairs their ability to get on with their lives. Recently, for example, I listened to a woman, divorced nearly five years, speak passionately about the importance of her divorce group in her life, about how understanding the other women are, how helpful. But no one had pushed and prodded her to get her professional life on track, nor did anyone suggest it was time for an end to mourning. When I expressed surprise that she still felt her suffering so keenly so many years after her divorce, she replied, offended, "It takes a long time. There are women in the group who were divorced ten years ago, and they're still in pain."

On the other side is Karen Richards, whose nineteen-year-old daughter was killed in an automobile crash a few years ago. Searching for surcease from her agony, she sought support in a group for parents who had lost their children. "They were very kind," she recalls, "and I don't want to criticize them. People have to deal with that kind of tragedy in their own way. But after a few meetings, I couldn't go back. There was so much pain and sadness in the room, I didn't think it was helping me. There were people there whose children died years ago, and they were grieving as if it happened yesterday. I wanted to die when Jennifer was killed; it would have been fine with me if I had. But I didn't want to *live* that way."

The stories that follow are tales of triumph over the past, life histories of women and men who refuse to be bowed by their trials, no matter how harsh and painful they may be. How does it happen that way? What makes it possible for some people to recover each time they fall, while others lie prostrate on the ground?

two

Sara Mikoulis: A Tale of Incest and Abandonment

I'VE WATCHED A LOT OF PEOPLE COME AND GO IN MY TWENTY-FIVE years of doing psychotherapy. Some people pass through quietly leaving few ripples behind; some so turbulently that it's not possible to forget them; and some remain in memory long after they've departed simply because the story they have to tell, and the courage and simplicity with which they tell it, is memorable. Sara Mikoulis is one of those people.

I met her about fifteen years ago when she came into therapy—a small, brown-skinned woman in her early thirties whose ready smile belied the depression underneath. The jeans and sweater she wore on that first visit revealed a slim, delicately boned body; her hair, pulled back in a pony tail, accented her finely wrought features.

From the outset I knew there was something special about her, some intangible quality that communicated an inner strength and a stubbornness that marked her a survivor—an impression that was soon confirmed by the story she told. For this was a woman whose past included everything from abandonment to brutality, incest, rape, poverty, and alcoholism. Yet when we met, she had just completed a twelve-year odyssey through college and graduate school while she also worked full time, mothered her daughter, and extricated herself from a brutal marriage. All with no help from anyone.

A therapist's days are filled with the need to shift focus and vision as each hour brings a different person and each person brings a particular history and a unique way of interpreting the events of a life. With experience those shifts become nearly automatic; you move from person to person with little thought or effort. But in the two years or so that Sara remained in therapy, I was never able to make that move easily because the contrast between her and the people who came on either side of her was so striking.

In the hour before, I saw a young man brought up in an upper middle-class professional family by parents who, by his own accounting, were demanding but also kind, loving, and supportive. He was, he said, "born to succeed." And until then he had: an Ivy League college, the best graduate school, an assistant professorship at a prestigious university. But he came into therapy so debilitated by anxiety about getting tenure that he couldn't do the work necessary to ensure it.

During the hour after Sara, I saw the thirty-something daughter of one of America's rich and powerful families who, although bright and talented, was unable to hold a job, was in a troubled marriage, and had difficulty nurturing her young son. She wanted very much to pull her life together, tried desperately hard to do so, but always seemed to fall short of her goals.

In between I listened to Sara Mikoulis, who told her story without drama or self-pity, who worried that being in therapy was self-indulgent, and who never failed to amaze me by her resilience. She seemed like one of those inflated toys that's built to retain its balance, the kind that, no matter how hard you hit it, bounces back to an upright position.

I heard from Sara from time to time after she left therapy. A Christmas card, a note reporting her progress, another telling me she was moving to Europe, news of her divorce, again when she returned to the United States after four years abroad. And with each one, the same thought: What makes some people able to overcome even the most malignant past while others with all kinds of advantage remain mired in it?

It seemed natural, then, that Sara Mikoulis came instantly to mind when I began to think about studying people who defy psychological expectations and transcend their past. We met for coffee; I explained the project. In her usual quiet and understated way, she couldn't understand why I thought there was anything special about the way she had lived her life. "It was hard," she acknowledged, "but it's just my life. What else was I supposed to do, lay down and die?" Nevertheless, she agreed to be interviewed partly because she wanted to help me, partly because she thought it might help her to deal with the problems that remain, and partly because she hoped that seeing her story in print would bring the resolution that had so far eluded her.

In each of our lives there are signal events, experiences over which we have no control, yet which profoundly shape the life ahead. Although Sara's story starts in infancy, she was seven years old when past and present collided in ways that would determine her future. As she speaks of that time, I see a delicate little girl, a paisley print dress covering her thin body, her coffee-colored skin gleaming in the southern sun. She stands in the front yard of a modest frame house in the "colored section" of a small Mississippi town, her bare feet planted firmly in the scrubby grass, and cries stubbornly, "No, I won't go."

A tall woman—a stranger dressed in city clothes—speaks in low, comforting tones as she reaches out to her, trying to make contact, to touch her, to get her to listen to an explanation she knows the child can't really comprehend. But Sara pulls away and runs to a woman who stands in the doorway squinting into the sun through tear-filled eyes. "I don't want to go with her," the child cries. "Why do I have to?"

"You just have to, that's all baby," the woman she's known all her life as *mama* says, stroking her hair gently as she speaks. "You have to go to your mama; she sent your Aunt Martha all the way down here to bring you back home," she explains, her voice choked with emotion.

Although today Sara is a competent and talented forty-five-year-old administrator in a social service agency who has traveled a long way from her Mississippi past, her voice rises in agitation as her words reawaken the pain and bewilderment she felt years ago. "I couldn't understand what they were saying to me," she recalls. "How could there be another mama who had some claim on me when this was the only mother I'd ever known? I came there when I was just a baby and didn't remember ever living anyplace else. This was my family and now there was this stranger who said she was my aunt come to take me back to people she said were my family. It didn't make sense. How could a little kid understand that?"

It's not unusual in black families for extended kin to pick up the pieces of a family in need. Sometimes a boy who's headed for trouble on the streets of the urban North is sent back to the family in the South in the hope that he'll "straighten up" in an environment with fewer temptations. Sometimes, as was true for Sara's mother, Geraldine Richardson, a divorce leaves a woman with children to support and no one to help with their care. So she sends them "down home" until she can figure out a way to manage.

In the Richardson family, however, only baby Sara was sent away. Her two-year-old brother, Andrew, stayed with his mother. "She says she couldn't take care of me, but she managed to keep my brother with her. He was always her boy; he was the one who counted," Sara says, the bitterness in her heart reflected in the harshness of her tone.

Perhaps Mrs. Richardson sent her baby away because she valued her son more than her daughter, as Sara believes. Perhaps it was because it was more difficult to arrange for the care of an infant than for a two-year-old. Perhaps it was for some combination of both these reasons—and more that we cannot know. Whatever the grounds for the choice her mother made when Sara was an infant, it was a defining event in the child's life.

When Sara speaks of her Mississippi years, the frown that furrowed her brow a moment earlier is erased, and her eyes grow distant as memory takes her back to that time. "Those were the best years of my life; they were the only happy years of my childhood."

It was, she says, the only time in her life she can remember feeling comfortable; the only time, too, she believed she was loved and felt she belonged. "It was the only real home I ever knew. My aunt and uncle never had any children of their own, so they were really happy to have me; they were my real mama and daddy."

Surrounded by loving parent surrogates, a grandmother who "fried chicken and made biscuits," and "lots of cousins and lots of toys," Sara blossomed in her Mississippi home. "I don't mean to make it sound idyllic," she warns. "They weren't well off or anything like that. In fact, they were kind of poor, and the house we lived in was little, real little. But my aunt kept it very clean, and she made it look as nice as it could."

She stops talking and stares out the window, her eyes distant, her expression sad. "You know, you take it for granted when you have a family that loves you and takes care of you. It's when you lose it, you realize what a gift it is. When I left Mississippi, I left all that behind me—being loved and cared for, I mean. That was the last time I ever felt like I belonged somewhere or like I fit in.

"My uncle had a little upholstery shop, and he used to take me to work with him. It seems like that was one of my main activities when I was real little; I think I was with him more than with my aunt. I don't know why; she didn't work. I don't ever remember them having any conversation about it, like her telling him to take me with him, or anything like that. I think he just liked the company."

Sara played around the shop while her uncle worked, climbing over the half-finished furniture that filled the tiny space, playing hide-and-seek among the bolts of fabric. When she got restless, her uncle would give her a few coins to buy a gingerbread loaf at the store down the street. Lunchtime found them walking hand in hand back to the house where her aunt had a meal waiting. At the end of the day her uncle used scraps of whatever fabric he had around to make her a special treat—a new rag doll to add to her collection. "I remember sitting there jiggling impatiently because I couldn't wait to see what kind of doll I'd get that day."

All that ended on the day Aunt Martha came to take her away. "In some ways the worst thing about all this is that it made a terrible breech between my aunt and uncle and me. I felt rejected and abandoned because they sent me away, so I was very, very angry at them." Anger that ran so deep, perhaps, because it was the second abandonment of her young life—the first when her mother sent Sara away, the second when she took her back.

"I know, I know," she continues, as if responding to my unspoken thoughts. "They didn't *send* me away; they had no choice. Now I can understand that they must have felt like they lost their only child because that's what I was to them—their child. But what does a seven-year-old kid know? As far as that little kid was concerned, they sent her away, so she was scared and mad and hurt and didn't want anything to do with them. Then they were hurt, I guess, because they felt like I rejected them.

"It was a mess. I didn't see them again until years later when my grandmother died and I went down for the funeral. I was grown by then, but so many terrible things had happened in my life, I still couldn't get past the bitterness."

Amid tears and protests, Sara and her Aunt Martha boarded the train that would take them north to Sacramento, California, where her mother, who had recently remarried, her stepfather, and her brother were awaiting her arrival. "I was so scared the only thing I remember about the trip was getting on the train there and getting off here and finding all those strange people looking me over. All I could do was cling to my aunt. It's crazy, isn't it? I didn't know her until she came for me in Mississippi, but by the time we got here, she felt like my lifeline."

From the moment of her arrival, there was trouble. Her brother, unaccustomed to a rival for his mother's attention, made it clear that she was unwelcome. "I don't think he even knew he had a sister until I turned up. Then, all of a sudden, he had to share his mother *and* his room." As Sara recalls it, he tormented her mercilessly, pulling her hair, hitting and kicking her, throwing whatever came to his hands at her, telling her she didn't belong in the family, urging her to go back where she came from. "We hated each other our whole lives; it's a miracle we didn't kill each other. He'd get into a kind of crazy rage and pick up anything he could get his hands on and throw it at my head. I fought back, but he usually won."

Her mother, too, found endless reasons for dissatisfaction with her daughter. She wasn't properly appreciative of her mother's sacrifices; she didn't smile enough; she was a troublemaker; she was selfish; she was stubborn; she was ugly; she was too black; she was stupid; she couldn't be trusted—complaints that often ended in vicious beatings. "I'd have to take off all my clothes and stand there naked while she beat me with the buckle end of the belt until I bled."

Once, in an act of stubborn courage that marks so much of her later life and is surely one of the reasons for her transcendence, Sara grabbed the belt from her mother's hands and swore she'd kill her if she hit her one more time. "And I felt like I'd do it, too," she concludes, her old sense of humiliation and outrage palpable in the room.

For the first year of her life in Sacramento, all she could think about was getting back to her Mississippi home. "I was forever packing that one little bag I came with and trying to run away. But I had no money and no idea how to go anywhere. So I'd go outside and sit on the stairs with my little suitcase until eventually someone would come out and get me."

At the same time that she yearned to leave her new home, when she found herself alone on the city streets, she imagined that someone was following her, lying in wait to grab her and take her off to yet another unknown place. So she'd rush home and hide in the house in an attempt to thwart the strangers who seemed to dog her steps. Recalling those frightening moments, she explains, "I guess I thought if someone could appear out of the blue and take me away once, it could happen again."

Eventually there were three more children in the family—twin girls, who were born a little more than a year after Sara's return, and another boy, seven years later. But the other children were bystanders in the central conflict in the household, which was between Sara; her brother, Andrew; and her mother. "No matter what he did, my mother blamed me. It was like I wasn't even her child."

It's hard not to wonder, as I listen to Sara, *What makes a mother reclaim her child then treat her so badly?* We can't know for sure, of course, but one thing seems clear: Sara's return threatened whatever equilibrium Geraldine Richardson's newly created family had achieved by then. The daughter she sent away in infancy came back a frightened, bewildered, and unhappy stranger who stubbornly refused to be grateful for her return. Her beloved son was enraged by his sister's reappearance, and the conflict between them was a constant source of disruption in the family. Her new husband, perplexed by his wife's treatment of her daughter, sometimes interceded in the child's behalf. "Even my stepfather saw how unfair she was to me," recalls Sara, "and eventually it was like I became his child."

But her stepfather's intercession came with a price. Most immediately, it aroused her mother's jealousy, which escalated her rage and with it, her reprisals. Worse yet, what may have started as normal human concern for a child who was being abused soon turned to something more. By the time Sara was nine years old, her stepfather was buying her little gifts, among them "cute little underthings and things like that," and helping her take a bath. "I didn't like him bathing me; it was creepy," Sara recalls, her lips curling in distaste. "I told my mother that I didn't like it and it didn't feel right, but she paid me no mind."

It wasn't long before "bathing" turned openly to fondling. Desperate for some relief from her stepfather's attentions, she told a teacher. But when confronted with her daughter's story, Mrs. Richardson turned a blind eye to what was the beginning of a long and painful incestuous relationship. "My mother was very angry at me when the teacher called them and asked them to come to school. When they came and she told them what I had said, they totally dismissed it and said she shouldn't pay any attention to me because I had a vivid imagination and was always telling lies.

"But I didn't give up because pretty soon he wasn't just fondling me. So a few months later I ran away and went to the police station to tell them what he was doing. They treated me like a runaway and called my parents. I don't know what they told the police when they came to get me because I wasn't in the room, but the cops just sent me back home with them."

As the months wore on, her stepfather's behavior progressed from fondling to demands for specific sexual acts—masturbation at first, then fellatio, and finally full sexual intercourse. "It's not possible that my mother didn't know what was going on," says Sara. "All of a sudden she started to make me douche with a solution of Hexall [a powerful disinfectant not made for internal use]. It was awful; she'd fix it so that it burned like hell. She'd stand over me and make sure I did it, like I was a filthy kid who needed to be punished. It wasn't like a mother teaching a daughter how to take care of her body. It was cruel, plain unadulterated cruelty. I couldn't have been that dirty that I had to be cleaned out that way, now could I?

"It was about that same time that she said my panties couldn't be washed in the machine with everyone else's clothes. I had to wash them in private and by hand—not my undershirt or my socks, only my underpants. She didn't do it to my sisters, only to me. Now why would she do that if she didn't know something was going on?"

As difficult as the incestuous relationship with her stepfather was, as much as it filled her with guilt, shame, and self-hatred, he was also the only one in the family who treated her with some kindness and regard. Except for her stepfather, Sara says, she was "totally estranged and isolated," an outcast who wasn't fit to associate with others in the family. "My mother treated me like a pariah. A lot of the time she wouldn't let the other kids talk to me, and I wasn't allowed to come to the table to eat with the rest of the family."

Characteristically, when Sara reflects on her relationship with her stepfather, she sees beyond her own victimization, an ability that's central to the process of transcendence. Without denying the damage he inflicted or her justifiable anger, she's able to grasp the complexity of their interaction. "It's interesting and complicated when I think about it now. It's true that he sexually abused me, but he never struck me. It was my mother who'd beat me until I bled, not him. He was the only one who showed any interest in me and treated me like a human being.

"My mother dressed the twins up real cute, the most beautiful coats, darling little socks, and Mary Jane shoes. But with me, it was like nobody cared. She either bought me tomboy things or ugly things that were too long and too big. But my stepfather would buy me all these frilly little things. I remember once he brought me these bright red panties with ruffles.

"It was seductive, him being nice to me when she was so cruel and I felt so alone. I felt ugly and unlovable all the time; then he'd come along and tell me I was pretty and call me his little princess—that was his pet name for me. I don't know, I think maybe I felt I owed him something in return," she says reflectively. Then, before the words have time to settle in the room, she adds passionately, "But I also hated him and what he was doing; it's just that there was no way out.

How could there be when I kept trying to tell people and nobody listened or cared?

"I always had the feeling that my mother had given me to him, that he actually owned me, as if she'd said, 'She's yours; you can have her.' I felt like I was his payment for staying in the family. So I felt he had a right to do what he was doing. After all, I was his."

Whatever her ambivalence about her stepfather, Sara had none about her brother, Andrew, who, having caught father and daughter in the act, made his own claim on Sara's body. "I hated him," she says flatly, her anguished rage still burning brightly. "He made my life a living hell from the time I arrived, and now he was blackmailing me. He said he'd tell everybody, not just my mother but the kids at school, and then they'd all know what kind of slut I was. I was only about ten years old then, and I was terrified of the humiliation. I begged him not to talk about it, but he just laughed. His price for not telling was to demand that I have sex with him."

She tried to tell her mother about her brother's sexual overtures, but once again Mrs. Richardson refused to listen, accusing Sara of being an incorrigible troublemaker. Frightened, with no place to turn, she gave in, but never without a fight. "There was always violence between me and Andrew—fighting, kicking, clawing. I actually tried to castrate him a couple of times, once with a hammer. But he was bigger and could always overpower me. It wasn't intercourse; it was *rape*."

By the time she was ten years old, Sara was being raped regularly by both her brother and stepfather. "I used to have fantasies where I'd literally stitch myself up so they couldn't get to me. Or I'd pray that I'd somehow turn into a boy so they'd leave me alone. For years I couldn't dress in a way that looked the least bit feminine because I was afraid of attracting that kind of attention. I still prefer unisex clothes like jeans and things."

She fought her brother and pleaded with her stepfather. I'd tell him I don't want to do it or tell him to stop because he was hurting me. But he'd pin my arms and tell me to just be quiet and relax, that it would be all right, that he loved me and wouldn't hurt me.

"It's outrageous. I felt like an object, not an individual, something to be done with as they wanted. What gives someone the right to do that to a child, to violate a person that way?" she asks indignantly. "I know I gave in, but there was always something gnawing at me. My piece—who I was and what I wanted, my real participation—was missing.

"I always felt so dirty. I'd wash and wash and wash, but nothing could take away the feeling. I had nightmares about it for years and years. I think about it now and wonder what it would have been like to have had a choice about when and how you'd have sex for the first time. I was cheated; I never had a chance to make that decision."

She finally was able to stop her brother a couple of years later, but only after he'd lured her into a vacant garage where he and three other neighborhood boys lay in wait and gang raped her. When she stumbled home a few hours later, her face filthy, her hair disheveled, her clothes torn, she was beaten for being late. She protested and tried to tell her parents what Andrew had done, but her mother slapped her and called her a liar. Even her stepfather didn't believe her, insisting piously that no brother would be party to such an outrage.

Before the gang rape, she says, she felt that there was no escape, that she had no choice but to give in to her fate. Afterward, perhaps because of her stepfather's betrayal, something inside her shifted. It was as if she finally understood fully and unequivocally that she could count on no one but herself. A terrible knowledge for a twelve-year-old, but one ultimately that helped her, not just to survive but to overcome. "I learned then that even when something's really hard, I can do what I have to do," she says with a broad smile that doesn't negate the steely determination that lies beneath her words. "It's the story of my life. I want to fit, but I can't. I want to do, but I can't. But that doesn't make me not do something. It only means I have to figure out a way to do it."

"Doing it" in this case meant keeping her brother out of her bed—

a feat she accomplished by becoming armed and dangerous. For the rest of the time she lived in that house, she slept fully clothed, except for her shoes, and kept a hammer under her pillow, which she wielded wildly at any sign of Andrew's approach. "I hit him with the hammer a couple of times, and that finally stopped him.

"After that, he went after the twins. He raped every one of us in the family, even my little brother. It was good practice for what he'd become later," she says, her eyes blazing, her words etched in loathing. "The last I heard of him was maybe fifteen years ago, and he was in the penitentiary in Arkansas, doing time for his second rape conviction. The first one was a few years earlier, right here in Sacramento." Her eyes turn sad, her brow furrows as if she's still trying to comprehend the incomprehensible. "You know," she says quietly, "even when my mother saw it in black and white in the newspaper and it said he was practically caught in the act, she never believed it."

Two years later, when Sara was fourteen, she stopped her stepfather as well. She had come home from school and, thinking she was alone in the house, went into the kitchen to get something to eat. Quietly he came up behind her and laid a hand on her breast. "I don't know what happened; it's like I went crazy," recalls Sara, shaking her head as if she still can't believe what she did. "I had a knife in my hand because I was fixing a sandwich, and I turned on him and tried to kill him. I didn't care about anything. I knew this was it; this was never going to happen to me again, no matter what the risk.

"I don't know where the strength came from; it was almost superhuman. We were on the floor in a full-fledged physical brawl, fighting like two men, wrestling back and forth, and me lashing out with the knife. But he was bigger and stronger and finally overcame me."

After he subdued Sara, her stepfather called her mother, who came home from work immediately. Frightened and miserable, Sara tried to tell her story, only to be rendered silent and invisible again. "All I wanted was just once for her to see me and to be able to tell my side. But it's like she was deaf and blind when it came to me. There I was, sitting in a chair and shaking because I was so scared, and all she could do was tell me to shut up. Then they went into the next room and closed the door."

A few minutes later, Mrs. Richardson emerged, looking, in Sara's words, "cold as ice," and said, "Both of us cannot live in this household, and I'm not going anyplace." For Sara, her worst nightmare had come true. She was about to be sent away once again. "No matter how long I live, I'll never forget those words," she says, repeating them softly as if to burn them into her memory.

A week later, she was on a train to St. Louis, dispatched to live with her biological father—a man she had never seen—and his new family. "That train ride was like a replay of the ride from Mississippi to Sacramento. There I was, going someplace I didn't know to people I'd never seen."

Compared to life in Sacramento, the years in St. Louis were relatively benign, although her father was hospitalized with a severe clinical depression within weeks after her arrival and remained depressed for most of her years there. Her stepmother, left to fend for herself with a young child and a moody adolescent stepdaughter she hardly knew, was kind enough but immersed in her own troubles. In this environment Sara sought refuge in books and school. "I spent a lot of time taking the bus to the library. That was my pattern; it still is. I find something to throw myself into that keeps me engaged in something besides my own worries. At that time it was school and reading whatever I could get my hands on."

This is one of the qualities shared by all the women and men in this book—the ability to see a world beyond their pain and to reach for something in it that validated and affirmed them. For Sara it was books, where she found solace and escape; and school, where her performance had already gained the admiration and appreciation of those in authority. Such activities, and the successes they brought, enabled her to retain a hold, even if only a tenuous one, on a sense of herself that was different from the one she saw reflected in the family mirror.

Her interest in psychology grew during these years, partly, she says, out of her fears about her own sanity. "I would go visit my father at the state hospital and see all those people there, and I kept wondering why they had such problems. I guess I was especially interested because I was afraid it was hereditary, and with a mother and father like I had, I worried that I was crazy, too. Besides, my mother always told me I was crazy."

In her characteristic way, she didn't succumb to her fears but determined to find out as much as she could in order to conquer them. It's this very capacity, this willingness to acknowledge her fears and seek ways to master them, that partly accounts for Sara's ability to transcend her past.

At eighteen she graduated from high school and returned to Sacramento. *Why, I wondered, would she go back to the place where she had suffered so much pain?* The question stops her; she looks at me blankly for a few moments, then says slowly, "I don't know: I guess because it was home."

Given her experiences there, however, it's unlikely that all she wanted was to go home. It would seem, instead, that she went back because, despite all she had suffered, she wasn't ready yet to give up on her family. Somewhere inside the hope still lived that she could make peace with her mother, that this woman who had borne her would see, finally, that Sara was worthy of her love and concern.

It wasn't simply a wild fantasy. It was fed by the fact that, by then, her stepfather, after having discovered that his wife was involved in a love affair with a woman, had taken the three younger children and left the marriage. Without him on the scene, Sara thought, she and her mother might find a way to relate differently to each other.

On her return, therefore, she got a job at the same place where her mother worked—the first step, she hoped, in the task of reordering their relationship. For a short while, it seemed to work, perhaps because Geraldine Richardson had no one else to turn to. Her husband and her other children were gone. Although her relationship with the woman continued, she was unable to come out as a lesbian and own it publicly. So she lived alone and embittered, turning more and more to alcohol to ease her distress. In this situation, Sara's presence in her life, if not in her house, may have been comforting.

But whatever brief peace mother and daughter achieved couldn't survive Mrs. Richardson's deep-seated antagonism for Sara. And they were soon caught in conflict again. For Sara it was another disappointment, another difficult moment in her history with her mother. Having tried and failed, however, she was more ready to put away her illusions about fixing the problems between them and more able to turn her attention to fixing herself. Accordingly, she changed her job, started to take courses at a local junior college, and began to take the next steps in the long struggle to transcend her past. But not without falling down and getting up several more times.

Not surprisingly, Sara's relationships with men remained difficult, troubled, and marked by brutality. Women who have had cruel or incestuous relationships with a parent in childhood often unconsciously seek out partners in adulthood with whom they replay the past. It isn't that they want to be brutalized again. Rather, it's a doomed attempt at mastery, an effort to relive the past in the hope of making it come out differently this time. It's a vain hope, of course, destined to fail until they are able to choose a different kind of man.

But Sara wasn't yet ready to do that. Shortly after her return to California, therefore, she became involved with George Allen, the man who would father her daughter, Amanda. George was, she says, an immature, dependent, and violent young man who couldn't provide for his family, yet was so wildly possessive that he couldn't tolerate

Sara leaving the house to go to work, let alone to school. "I was with him for a few years, but it was an ugly relationship," she says with disgust. "He was terribly violent and very possessive. He didn't want me to go to school or work or anything, yet he couldn't support himself, let alone me and the baby. We were always fighting—every time I walked out of the house—because he was so suspicious. And he would beat up on me all the time. But he couldn't stop me," she says, the defiance she felt then evident in the words she speaks now.

Why did she stay? For Sara, still only a little past her twentieth year, the physical, sexual, and emotional violence that marked her relationship with George was so much a part of her experience that it seemed normal, as if this was as much as she could expect in life. "It wasn't so different from my mother's house," she says acidly.

There was also something else that kept her there, however, something that was connected to her striving for emotional health, to her openness to relationships that could help to repair the wounds inside her. She had met George when she became friends with his mother, Norma, one of the several women in her adult life who, at different times, became her mother surrogates. Leaving him meant severing her attachment to a woman who offered the warmth, comfort, and acceptance she yearned for. "His mother was his saving grace. She and I were really good friends; I hated to lose her, too. It seems like I've had so many losses in my life, and I don't do loss well, even now," she says, struggling to hold back tears.

"Before Norma I got really close to my landlady, a wonderful Jamaican lady. She was very good to me, like a surrogate mother, and I really cared for her a lot. Unfortunately, not long after we met, she became ill with stomach cancer, and I watched her die. That was one of the hardest things I ever did in my life. It was a terrible loss. I knew if I left George, I'd lose Norma, too, and after my landlady-mother, it was too hard."

Finally, however, when Amanda was still only a few months old, George's violence became intolerable, and Sara fled. "We had this huge fight with him beating me up and screaming at me that I better behave. Then he left. As soon as he was out the door, I packed everything Amanda and I owned and got out as fast as I could."

It's no surprise that the early years of her daughter's life weren't easy for Sara. For a woman who had been so ill nurtured for so long, whose own dependency needs had been ignored from the time she was seven years old, the extreme dependency of an infant raised excruciatingly painful feelings of deprivation. "Sometimes I'd get so overwhelmed and feel so angry, I was terrified I'd hurt her like my mother hurt me.

"When she was an infant, I compensated by being overly involved," she says, speaking haltingly, as if each word is a painful reminder of feelings she'd rather forget. "But when she began to move around and walk and would get into things like babies and toddlers do, I'd sometimes lose it. I can't believe I did it, but I actually hit her with a belt a couple of times, just like my mother did to me," she admits, burying her head in her hands as if to shield herself from her own censorious thoughts—and undoubtedly from those she imagines I hold as well. Then, after a moment, she looks up and, tears streaming down her face, asks, "How can you know how to take care of a child in a loving way when you didn't have that in your own life?"

She did have that, of course, when she lived with her aunt and uncle in Mississippi in the years between one and seven. Why does she erase those years now? Partly they're obliterated because they ended in what felt to her like an abandonment, one that was doubly painful because it came on top of an earlier loss when her mother sent her away. And partly those early experiences are wiped out of her emotional memory because the years that followed were so cruel.

It's likely that the time in Mississippi could have overcome the effects of the abandonment of her first year if her aunt and uncle—the people she came to call her parents—had not been forced to send her away as well. It's also likely that she could have managed the second rupture with less emotional damage if she had exchanged one loving family for another. Instead, the two came together, the second abandonment of her young life—this time by her beloved "parents"—and the brutality and sexual exploitation she met in her new family. Together, they left her badly scarred and acutely vulnerable to feelings of rejection and abandonment.

Some people simply sink into the pain of such feelings. Others, like Sara, cover the pain over with anger—a common psychological defense that, in her case, has been functional in some ways, dysfunctional in others. It's functional in that her anger has mobilized her and kept her from becoming trapped in victimhood; dysfunctional in that it has allowed her to expunge the good years in Mississippi from her inner life.

It isn't that she's unaware of those years or denies the happiness and security she felt then. Cognitively, she recalls the time with genuine warmth. But the pain of the rupture was so great that she still can't consistently hold those good years—and the people who made them so—in her emotional memory.

Within a year after Sara left George, she met and married Rick Johnson. "There was this drive in me to be involved with a healthy male, and I thought maybe this was it. He was a good-looking black man, dressed real sophisticated, not hip, not slick, not looking like a hustler, but really well groomed. He had a business; he seemed to be a solid citizen. I thought I'd be living a fairy tale, but he turned out to be worse than the rest. He was a drug dealer and a killer. He abused me really badly, and I was terrified of him."

She pauses, shifts uncomfortably in her chair, then with words that demonstrate a seasoned understanding of the difference—or lack of it—between herself and her prostitute sister, she continues, "You know, my sister, Margo, got involved with someone who put her on the streets, and I used to think, *Thank God I never did that*. Well, now I know I did do it, but I was never out there on the street or in a brothel. My way was more sophisticated; I did it under the guise of being in a relationship."

Soon after she married Rick, Sara became pregnant and was forced against her will to carry the baby to term. "The doctor insisted that he wouldn't do an abortion without my husband's consent. But when I mentioned it to Rick, I thought he'd kill me on the spot. After that he became even more abusive than he was before, and I got severely depressed. I knew it would be a disaster to have this baby, but I had no way out. I tried to starve myself; I inserted things inside me to try to abort; I drank two bottles of castor oil and endless bottles of mineral oil. But nothing happened."

After the birth of her son, the abuse escalated. "He'd come back in the middle of the night from whatever he was doing and drag me out of bed and throw me around the house. I never knew why." But she stayed, partly because she had no money and nowhere to go; partly because she continued to hope he would change, that she could be good enough, loving enough, kind enough to make a difference; and partly because she still had not fully shaken the belief that this was her destiny, the one she deserved.

But this is also the same woman who, as an adolescent, grabbed the belt from her mother's hand, the same one who stopped her brother with a hammer and her stepfather with a knife. So she finally broke free but, as in her earlier life, not until the violence became unendurable. "The last time, that was it. My son was still just a baby when Rick came home one night, shook Amanda awake and took her out of bed, then dragged me by the hair to the bathroom, where he pushed me down on the toilet and beat me with a pistol.

"Amanda was crying and trying to hide her eyes, but he made her watch while he put the gun in my mouth and threatened to blow my head off. I think I must have passed out because I don't remember what happened after that. All I remember is that he was gone when I came to, and I knew I had to get away. I was so badly beaten up I could hardly move, but I grabbed Amanda and the baby and flew out of the house."

The saga of Rick and Sara didn't end there, however. He hunted her, threatened her, harassed her, stalked her, and finally broke into her apartment and kidnaped the baby. For the first time in the many hours we spoke together, Sara's affect became almost totally flat, her voice nearly toneless as she told of being forced to give up her son. "The police made him give the baby back. Then there was a custody battle, which I won, but I knew it would never end. He said he'd kill me if I didn't let him have my son, and he meant it. So after fighting him for about a year and living in terror, I went to court and totally relinquished custody of that child. It was the only way out. Except for a court-arranged visit a few months later, that was the last time I laid eyes on him."

She stares into space wordlessly for a few moments, then, with a small shudder, continues, "Only recently I cringed and felt like my body actually jerked around when I realized that I'd played out the same scenario with my son that my mother did with me, only this time it was the boy who got sent away and the girl who got kept. But I tell you, even now when I think about having to deal with Rick again, it's like no time has elapsed. I'm as scared now as I was then."

Remarkably, no matter what the problems in her family life during these years, Sara never stopped working and going to school. "That was the only thing that saved me during that time," she says. "When I was with George, I was going to junior college and working in a halfway house for men who had been institutionalized. After I left him, I got a job working at night, the graveyard shift, in another halfway house, but this one was for single mothers. I'd go to classes in the daytime and bring Amanda with me to work at night, and she'd sleep there while I was on shift.

"That's when I got my AA degree and was accepted to this private university, where I went for two years. But it cost so much money to go there that I couldn't afford it after that, so I transferred to the state college, which is where I finished my bachelor's and got my master's degree."

Sara's third try at a relationship with a man proved to be an important turning point, not just for her but for her daughter as well. She met Gregory Mikoulis, a successful white professional man, when she was in her last year of graduate school. The attraction, she says, was instantaneous, and they were married a few months after she completed her training.

As I listen to Sara talk about her marriage to a white man, I'm struck by how little she has to say on the subject of being black in America. When pushed, she explains, "When I was a kid, I didn't think about race. I know it's hard to understand, but in my mind I was always invisible. I thought people didn't see me; I was like a ghost. So even if racial issues came up when I was younger, I didn't really notice. It sounds weird, I know, but I had no consciousness of being different in terms of race. I knew I was different, but it had to do with who I was in the family and in the world, not with race."

For a child whose central life trauma was in the family, who was the despised outsider there, the "otherness" of race—and whatever stigma attached to it—seemed irrelevant, no different from what she already experienced at home. "I don't mean that race wasn't a real issue; it's just that I didn't interpret it that way then," Sara continues. "I knew about the civil rights movement, of course, but I didn't think it had anything to do with me or that it would benefit me in any way. I know this sounds kind of crazy, but I never attached any of it to anything personal in my own life.

"We were the first black kids to go to our junior high school, and I remember being bused there and not being able to participate in some things. But I didn't put it down to race. If I wasn't able to participate in things at school, it was no different from how things were at home. I was invisible and unwanted wherever I went. So it all fit very neatly, and race didn't seem to be the reason. It was just that I was me, and that's what I deserved."

It's not a surprise, then, that when asked whether she had any reservations about an interracial marriage, she shrugs, "The black-white thing was never an issue between me and Greg. After we were married, it sometimes bothered me that he saw nothing redeeming in black culture. We'd talk about it sometimes, but I accepted that's how he was. He was giving us so much, I couldn't very well get picky about him not wanting to go to a black fair or something, could I?"

Obviously, however, the marriage between a black woman and a white man was not irrelevant to others. "If we were aware of it, it was because other people made us aware," continues Sara. "My family made a big deal about it. They were mad; they thought I had sold out. But I didn't have much connection with them by then, and what they thought didn't matter to me."

By contrast, Greg's widowed mother, a first-generation Greek immigrant, surprised Sara by welcoming her warmly when they met. For a woman who had for so long stood outside the family fold, who knew so intimately the bitter taste of her own mother's aversion, it was nearly unbelievable to find herself basking in the acceptance of this family she would soon call her own.

To marry Greg, she had to be baptized in the Greek Orthodox Church, a sacrament she accepted partly because it seemed a small return for the kindness his mother had bestowed upon her, and partly because it offered the possibility for a new identity and, along with it, a new life. As a child Sara had been unable to believe in a church that embraced her mother, so she rejected religion and refused to be baptized. "I was the only one in the family who wasn't baptized. It was the one thing they couldn't force me to do."

At the time, her determined refusal was another display of the kind of stubborn courage that made her life in the family more difficult and that also ultimately saved her sanity. For she wasn't simply refusing baptism. It was a step, even if not consciously understood at the time, in the process of rejecting an identification with the family, a move that not only affirmed her marginality but, painful though it was, embraced it as she searched for a self that was independent of their definition of her.

When, later in life, she was faced with the idea of being baptized in the Orthodox Church, it became more than just another step away from her family. "It was," she says, "like a rebirth," the culmination of a lifelong search for something she could believe in, for a place where her emerging identity—a sense of self that wasn't based on her pained and flawed past—would be accepted and nurtured.

Although her marriage to Greg was not without difficulties, it bore none of the misery and brutality of her past. Greg, who had not had any children, eagerly embraced Amanda as his own, becoming the only real father she had ever known. "He was wonderful," Sara says with a smile. "It was the first time in my life I was with someone who accepted me completely, not just me but my daughter, too. He made a better life for us, a truly better life, better than anything I ever dreamed about."

The good life he provided notwithstanding, this marriage, too, ended in divorce a decade or so later. "Greg and I still love each other; we always will," says Sara wistfully. "But I couldn't get past my anger. The problem is, it was never clear who I was angry at. I mean, there were reasons to be angry at Greg, but I also kept getting the lines mixed up. Half the time I didn't know if I was angry at my step-father or my husband. The lines between the past and the present were so confused, I couldn't separate them out. We were together a long time, but finally we knew it had to end."

With the failure of her marriage to Greg, the legacy of Sara's past came back to haunt her, this time in a new way. Until then, she and Amanda, who was about seventeen by then, were a tight twosome, connected by a shared life, a mother's sense of responsibility, and Sara's determination not to repeat her own past with her daughter. As she contemplated the separation from Greg, however, she was overcome by the old sorrow. Although the divorce was mutually agreed upon, she felt rejected and abandoned once again. Surely, she thought, there must still be something terribly wrong inside her if she couldn't manage a life with a good man like Greg. Where, she wondered, would she ever belong, ever feel comfortable?

During her years with Greg, they had taken regular trips to Greece, the country of his parents' birth to which he remains deeply attached. "Greg had always planned to retire there, so we used to go there on vacations and stay a couple of months sometimes. I was very excited by it and began to study the language and the culture. It was one of those things I could immerse myself in and forget about everything else.

"I loved Greece from the first time I went. I don't know why," she says, shaking her head as if her response is still a mystery to her. "It's just that something there made me feel at home, like I belonged, like maybe I could actually fit."

These are powerful feelings for someone who had never fit, seductive enough so that once the marriage ended, all she could think of was fleeing to Greece. But what of Amanda, the child she was so proud of, the one she had tried so hard to protect from the grief of abandonment? In that moment, nothing mattered but her escape—not from Amanda, not from Greg, but from herself and the terrible feelings inside her. "I was depressed, frightened, feeling unprotected, and I had to get away. I'm not proud of it now, but then it didn't matter that Amanda had a year left in high school; I *had* to go. I knew Greg loved her and would take good care of her, so I guess I told myself she'd be fine with him," she says ruefully.

"I tried to explain to her, but what could I say that she'd understand? Nothing! How do you explain to your child that you're going to do something so totally selfish? She was absolutely uncomprehending. She didn't *want* to understand. She was confused, hurt, disappointed in me, and very, very angry"—anger and hurt that would take years to mend.

Sara stops talking for a moment, her eyes fixed on her hands in her lap. Then, her voice choked with tears, she continues, "It was very hard on Amanda, I know that. But for me, Greece was paradise because I could get away from my past. Nobody knew anything about me; it was a fresh start. Here there's no escape from the past; there are reminders wherever I go—people and places that don't let you forget. And you know how it is, you get defined and labeled as a certain kind of person early on, and then people expect you to behave that way. Even if you want it to be different—or even if you actually *are* different—they don't really give you a chance because they don't see you. They only see the person they have in their minds. In Greece I had no history, so nobody had a stake in keeping me in a certain box."

The experience of dealing with people who need to keep us in "a certain box" is familiar to many of us. We live it each time we go "home" to find a family who can't see and credit the person who stands before them. Instead, the stamp we bore as children remains indelible in their vision. The generosity of the child who was defined as selfish goes unnoticed and unrewarded. The one who was labeled stubborn and difficult is seen that way, no matter how cooperative she may now appear.

In this context, the old designations and role assignments often become a self-fulfilling prophecy. We become what they say we are, at least when in their presence. It's to affirm our adult selves, to see ourselves without the baggage of our past, that we distance ourselves, physically and psychologically, from the family and community of our childhood.

For Sara, then, leaving the country was a chance to find and develop parts of herself that had been denied for so long. "I could be anything I wanted; I could write a whole new script," she says. In exchanging the clamor of urban life in California for the rural serenity of a village in Greece, she could construct another definition of self, a "new script" for her life among people who hadn't yet "defined and labeled" her. In putting herself in a position where she was forced to learn new customs, speak another language, form different kinds of relationships, she stripped herself of all she knew, indeed, of all she had been, and opened the way to the further development of the woman she was in the process of becoming.

Of the relationships she found in Greece, the most important was with Maria, an older woman who adopted Sara as her own. Maria introduced her into the community and helped her to find work, even though it was illegal to hold a job on a visitor's visa. Like a good mother, Maria worried that Sara wasn't eating enough and insisted that she have dinner with the family so they could watch over her intake. "She was the mother I dreamed of having," says Sara. "She was always there and ready to help. I had moved from Athens to this little village—the only black person on the island—and Maria took me under her wing and taught me the things I needed to know to get along in that strange culture. She took me around and introduced me to everybody to make sure I'd be totally accepted. And I was.

"I didn't need to prove anything to her. She saw me, I mean, the me my own mother never could see, and she liked me for who I was. When I tried to tell her about my unwholesome background and some of the terrible things I'd done, all she said was, 'I don't care about any of that. I can see into your soul, and I know you're a good person.' Can you imagine what that was like for me? Her generosity was overwhelming."

But it wasn't just Maria's warm, open heart that made this relationship possible. What cemented it is the quality I call *adoptability*—the ability to attract people and to use what they offer—that Sara has in abundance. For despite her past experiences and the legitimate anxieties they generated, she always remained open to those relationships that promised to heal her hurts and soothe her fears. Consequently, at every major turning point in her adult life, she found a surrogate mother—a woman who was kind, nurturing, and supportive; who validated, respected, and protected her; a woman whose constant and caring presence offered the reassurance that she might indeed be lovable. It's as if she had an inner radar that directed her toward women who could be the mother she longed for—radar developed perhaps out of her experience with her aunt in Mississippi, the woman who was the good mother of her early childhood.

"From the time I was eighteen and came back from St. Louis, there was some woman who came to my rescue," Sara says. "First, it was my wonderful Jamaican landlady. Most recently, it was Maria in Greece. It was terrible when I had to leave Greece because it meant leaving her, too."

If living in Greece was "paradise" and her relationship with Maria so important, why did she leave? Her reasons are mixed, not fully clear even to her. At the most obvious level, there was a question of her visa. She had been there on a tourist visa, which had to be renewed each year. As long as she was married to Greg, the Greek authorities assumed she had some means of financial support, although she never relied on him for money during that time. Once she was divorced, they wanted proof that she could support herself without violating the provisions of her visa, which didn't allow her to hold a paid job. Since she couldn't provide the documentation they demanded, they asked her to leave the country.

But, as everyone knows, there are ways around such bureaucratic requirements. People find them all the time. The fact that Sara never seriously sought a way out of her visa dilemma suggests that something else was going on, something that tugged at her, some unfinished business that pulled her back to these shores. That unfinished business was her daughter, Amanda, who was by then attending a prestigious university and making plans for her graduate education—all with Greg's financial and emotional support. It was Sara's turn, not just to be available to her daughter but to make amends.

"I'd like to go back to Greece for good one day, but I know I have to finish working out my life here," she now says. "I think it was devastating for both of them—Greg and Amanda—when I left. Greg picked up the pieces for her; he was her strength during that time. I owe him a lot, and I'll always be grateful. Now it's my turn to take care of them."

It's over three years now since Sara's return, years during which she devoted herself to repairing the breach with Amanda. "She was relieved when I came back, but she was also angry, very angry," Sara says. "I don't blame her. I was glad to be with her, but she knew I wasn't thrilled to be back here, so I'm sure there was some uncertainty in her mind. Was I staying or leaving? Was I back for good, or would I pick up and go away again? It took quite awhile before she could trust me again."

Although Sara doesn't discount the anguish she caused her daughter, she's proud of the relationship they have today. Whatever her lapses or failures as a mother, the generational chain has been broken. "I love that kid deeply, and she knows it. We have a really wonderful way of being with each other now," she says with a pleased smile. "I'm so proud of her. She's grown up to be a wonderful, special human being.

"We had some hard times when she was little, but I turned that around real fast. And it was real hard for her when I left for Greece, but we've come through that, too. What I can say now is that I finally feel healed enough so I won't ever have to hurt her again. And I think she knows and trusts that now."

Problems remain for Sara, of course. The scars of the past are still too easily opened. Although her mother has been dead for several years, her voice can still haunt Sara in ways that are damaging to her self-esteem. Consequently, she works at a job that doesn't tap her capacities, yet she's reluctant to risk going after something more appropriate to her talents. Relationships with men remain difficult, although she no longer tolerates any kind of abuse, whether verbal or physical.

From time to time what she calls her "dark side" emerges—periods when she feels anxious and depressed, when she fears that the marks on her soul are visible on her face. But these times come with much less frequency and intensity now, and she's learned, she says, "to honor those feelings," to know that they'll pass, and to find ways to nurture herself until they do.

Her feelings of marginality, the sense that she's always the outsider, remain. But she understands now that her marginality, bitter and lonely though it has been, also enabled her to reserve some part of herself, to keep that core of self safe from the assaults that threatened to destroy her if she joined her tormentors and identified with them. For it was her siblings, the children who were central in the family and who, therefore, identified with it, who were crushed by its pathology and descended into crime, prostitution, alcoholism, illegitimacy, and long-term welfare dependency.

three

Petar Steprovic: Son of the Infidel

I DON'T KNOW WHAT I WAS EXPECTING BEFORE I MET PETAR Steprovic, but it isn't what I see when he stands at the door of my hotel room, his briefcase in one hand, the finger of his other hooked into his coat, which is slung over his shoulder. We had been introduced on the telephone by a mutual friend who knows of my work and who suggested that Petar would be a good subject for this study. "He's a great guy, very interesting, very smart, but," my colleague warned, "he can be pretty sensitive." When I asked what "sensitive" meant, all I got was, "You know, sensitive, maybe a little unpredictable; tuned in to every nuance; don't worry, you'll manage it."

So although the several phone conversations necessary to explain the project and set up our meetings were easy enough, I remained somewhat apprehensive as I awaited the knock on the door that would signal our first face-to-face encounter. But my anxiety faded quickly when I looked into the open face of this big, solidly built man, with a disarmingly warm smile—a man whose churning energy and personal magnetism fill whatever space he inhabits.

From our earlier conversations, I already knew a little of his history and accomplishments. At thirty-nine, Petar, who had emigrated from Slovenia (in what was then Yugoslavia) when he was eight years old, has earned two master's degrees, a Ph.D., a Fulbright fellowship, and is the author of eight books. I knew, too, that, in addition to the dislocation of immigration and the anguish caused by a physical deformity, his past was shadowed by cruelty, alcoholism, mental illness, and death—events sufficiently traumatic that he remarked in one phone conversation, "If I hadn't separated myself from that family very early, I'd be in an insane asylum."

It's hard to believe, as we talk animatedly about the city we're both visiting, that this charismatic man could have been a neglected and rejected child. But his smile fades quickly, and the restless energy that seems to surround him quiets when I begin the interview by asking for the dominant memory of his early childhood. For several long moments he's silent and completely still, his head resting on the back of the small couch on which he's seated. Finally, his eyes on the ceiling, his voice tight with anguish, he begins to speak.

In his mind's eye, he's five years old again, a sturdy little boy who's being dragged along the street of a small Slovenian city by a tall, attractive woman, who holds him firmly by the hand as she strides determinedly forward. "Where are we going?" Petar asks his mother plaintively, his short legs churning to keep up the pace. But if she hears, she doesn't respond. Instead, she hurries on until they enter a long gray structure that's identifiable anywhere in the world as a government building.

The child looks around uneasily and asks, "Why are we here?"

"You'll see," she replies, speaking for the first time since they set out on their journey. She announces their arrival to a receptionist, then sits down on a bench a few feet away, waiting. He wriggles around impatiently as small children do. After what seems an interminable wait, an attendant arrives and ushers them into a room where dead bodies are laid out on long, narrow tables. He's frightened now, but his mother pulls him forward, holding tightly to his hand to prevent his escape. Halfway across the room they stop before a table on which lies the body of a man. "It was my father lying there naked and all blue," recalls Petar, the shock of the moment registering again on his mobile features. "That's how I found out he was dead. My mother didn't say a word, no explanation, nothing, only, 'There's your father,' as if I couldn't see for myself it was him."

Stunned, the little boy pulls away and rushes from the room crying. Outside the building, he finds himself in the middle of its long gravel driveway. "I was standing there crying; then for some reason I picked up some of the gravel. It's funny, isn't it," he remarks, "how you remember such details. I didn't throw it or anything; I just held it in my hand. And then my mother came up and hit me. To this day, I have absolutely no idea why. I suppose because I was crying, you know, being a kid who just saw his father dead. But she never wanted me to be a kid. Or," he concludes bitterly, "maybe I should just say she never wanted me.

"The whole thing with the funeral, that's another story," says Petar, now leaning forward as he warms to his tale. "I don't remember much about the funeral itself, but we had to take this long train ride to get there. And it seemed like the whole time we were on the train my mother was slapping me around. I don't know why. What could my crime have been? I was just a little kid.

"Then when we finally got to this village where the funeral would be, some people there offered us some food. But my mother said it was poisoned and wouldn't let me eat it. We hadn't had anything to eat for a long time, so I was hungry and began to cry. All I got was another whack."

Years later Petar asked his mother why she couldn't have found a kinder way to inform him of his father's death. "I wanted you to know he was dead," was all she would say. "I couldn't believe what I was hearing," he now says, "so I persisted, 'But I was only a child; how could you take me to the morgue to see his body like that?' She had no response, not a word, nothing."

When he finishes the story, Petar shifts restlessly in his seat as if to shake off the memory, then says quietly, "That's just the beginning; it gets worse." "Worse" came very quickly when his mother told him his father had committed suicide. "He was the only one in the family who was kind and loving to me. I couldn't believe he'd kill himself and leave me like that. It hurt just to think about it. Then there was my mother's family; they were a very Catholic bunch—I mean fanatical—and suicide was a big thing. So there was all this judgment about how he died."

It wasn't only in the family that harsh judgment was rendered. The Catholic community in which they lived was equally intolerant of suicide. By the time Petar returned from the funeral, therefore, the neighborhood was abuzz with shocked talk, and children who had been his friends treated him like a pariah. "It was as if I was infected with some bad spirit. The kids teased me; they threw stones at me. It was like I was contaminated by some kind of black magic."

Perhaps because he didn't want to believe it, but also because the circumstances were genuinely mysterious, Petar never fully accepted his mother's story of suicide. Many years later, when he returned to Slovenia, he inquired into the events surrounding his father's death. "I did a pretty thorough investigation and concluded that my father was probably murdered, although no one was ever apprehended."

Domagoj Steprovic and Maria Horvat, Petar's parents, met in a mental hospital. "He was an alcoholic, so he was in for detox. She was there because she was paranoid schizophrenic," their son explains. "She still goes in and out and can get very paranoid. It's something, isn't it," he says laughing self-consciously, "both my parents in a mental hospital. For a long time I worried about what that says about me."

Domagoj and Maria married soon after they were released from the hospital—a union doomed to an early failure. But by the time they separated, there were two children—Petar, who was still an infant, and a brother three years older who, after being ravaged by multiple sclerosis, died at twenty-two.

Custom in Slovenia at the time dictated that if a woman left her husband, she returned to her family. So Maria and her children moved into her parents' home, a move that only compounded Petar's misery. "Living in that house was a real hell," Petar recalls angrily. "My grandparents didn't like me any better than my mother did. They beat me up pretty badly, many times to the point of having welts all over my body. It's like I was identified as my father's son and was the outcast.

"All my life my mother told me my father was nothing but an alcoholic bum and that I'd grow up to be worthless, just like him. But I loved my father. He was the only bright spot in my life. I have nothing but nice memories of him; it's just the opposite with my mother. Before he died I was sometimes allowed to spend a weekend with him in his apartment. That was heaven," he says, his eyes soft and smiling as he remembers the good times. "There was no violence, no craziness, none of that bullshit, just nonstop good times. When I look at old photographs of me and him, I see myself looking like an ordinary happy kid. But in the pictures with her, I look like a frightened little animal."

The harshness of the child's situation with his mother, his conviction that his father was his only source of love and protection, made his death even harder to bear than it might otherwise have been. True, the glowing picture Petar now presents may well be the idealized memory of a five-year-old whose father's kindnesses stand out so vividly in contrast to his mother's cruelties. The elder Steprovic was, after all, a lifelong alcoholic, a condition not known for facilitating the kind of loving constancy a child needs. But this is one of those times in psychological life when the facts are not as important as the way the experience is internalized and remembered. And whatever the facts, it's the internal experience that made his father the good parent of Petar's life.

Now, as he recalls those years, he stands up and paces about the small room, his face set in hard lines. "Goddamn, remembering all this is hard; it really hurts," he says. "After my father died, there was no one for me. My mother's very paranoid and she's also crazy about Catholicism, a real religious fanatic. It's like it took over everything. She's so bad she even got into religious struggles with her parents and, believe me, they're plenty fanatical themselves.

"I've never been able to be comfortable in the Catholic church since then. My mother did that for me. I see the church, and Christian culture in general, as basically hostile because it has been so hostile to me."

But it isn't the church itself that has been hostile to Petar. It's his mother and her fanaticism. Her religious excesses didn't just dominate the daily life of the household, they determined her relationship with her son as well. Since her former husband didn't share her devotion to the faith, the fruit of that union was, for her, the child of an apostate, a despised infidel who, even in death, contaminated her home with the son he left behind. It was as if the child was the fruit of her sin in coupling with a defector from the faith, the cross she would bear forever in payment for her transgression. "I always thought her fanatical Catholicism had something to do with the way she treated me, like maybe I had some terrible flaw and could never be a good enough Catholic. She'd always remind me that I was my father's son, as if that was the worst crime in the world. It was clear that she didn't want me around, like I would pollute the atmosphere or something."

When Petar was eight years old, his mother married Michael Bancroft, a sergeant in the United States Army who was stationed nearby. "Things didn't get any better after they got married. He was a religious nut, too. But," he says, his voice rising in anger, "with all the religious bullshit in that family, they were the worst sort of hypocrites. There was no Christian charity in that house. It was filled with anger, shouting, and violence. My stepfather was an alcoholic who eventually died of cirrhosis of the liver. He was a very violent guy who would pin me up against the wall and punch me out when he got mad, which was often.

"You couldn't get away from religion in that family, not for a minute. We had to pray at every meal, go to mass every day, confession every week. It got so I ran out of sins to confess; the only thing I could say finally was that I hated my mother.

"It was really crazy. You'd do some innocent thing and it would be a catastrophe, like you committed some kind of a mortal sin. Even your thoughts weren't safe because they insisted that thinking sinful thoughts was just as terrible as doing bad things. The whole idea that you can sin by thinking is crazy. But what does a kid know? When I was real little, I'd sit there trying to monitor my thoughts. But even when I was doing that, I kind of knew this was part of the family craziness. So by the time I was nine or ten, I stopped paying attention, you know, just tried to tune them out. If I hadn't done that, I'd have gone crazy."

It's this ability to separate himself from the family pathology—his mother's paranoia, his stepfather's rage, the fanaticism of their religious belief—that enabled Petar to cope with the difficulties of life in the family of his childhood. In defining these behaviors as part of what he calls "the family craziness," he was able to distance himself, becoming an observer instead of a participant.

It's one of the paradoxical psychological realities that it can sometimes be more difficult to separate from a family that, on the surface, seems relatively benign—the mother who smiles while she exacts her own brand of retribution from the child, the father who never hits but silently withholds his acceptance and approval—than from parents whose rage and malevolence are unmistakable. A child in a family whose benevolent face masks the hostility roiling underneath often is caught by the mixed message, never fully certain that his perceptions are sound, mired in guilt over the unhappiness he thinks he caused. In a family where parental behavior is clearly brutal, it can be easier for a child to comprehend, even if only in some inchoate way, that the problem doesn't lie with him. Indeed, an important step in overcoming such a past is the child's ability to understand that the punishment is unjust, that it isn't his fault.

That understanding, however, comes with both a price and a prize. For Petar, the cost was isolation, loneliness, and the terrible knowledge that he was left to cope on his own long before he was ready. But his alienation, and his anger at the humiliations and injustices that were visited upon him, also left him free to think and act independently of the family pathology—free psychologically to resist their blows and their blame; free, too, to seek alternative sources of support and identification, which helped to liberate him from his family's damning estimate of him.

Shortly after the Bancrofts married, Michael's tour of duty in Slovenia ended, and the family moved across the sea. As Petar remembers that journey and its aftermath, he seems to turn into the eight-year-old he was then—his face set, his eyes hooded as if to cover over the ache in his heart, his voice edged with a harsh bitterness. "After we arrived here, my mother put a curtain over my Slovenian background. Slovenia was totally wiped out, like it didn't exist," he recalls. "We were only allowed to talk English in the house, and since I didn't know any English then, well, you can imagine, it wasn't easy. Then my mother forced me to take my stepfather's name. God, I hated both of them. But I had no choice, so I became Peter Bancroft."

Generations of immigrants to America have found themselves with new names, sometimes because an official at the port of entry couldn't pronounce and spell the names they had carried all their lives until then; sometimes because a teacher, a social worker, or a well-meaning sponsor decided to Americanize their names as a way of helping them to fit in. But a name isn't just a label or a tag to be put on and taken off at will. When we say our name, we are making a statement about our identity; it's who we are as surely as the color of our eyes and the shape of our bodies. To lose our name is to lose an important part of ourselves.

"I always felt like they were talking about someone else," recalls Petar, whose new name made him a stranger to himself. "They'd call that name, and I'd feel like I should turn around and see who they were talking to. As soon as I turned twenty-one, I changed my name back to Petar Steprovic. It was the first time in years I felt like me, like this is who I am."

On the inside, he refused to be Peter Bancroft, holding tight to his earlier name and the identity that went with it. On the outside, he functioned admirably in his new land, at least in the world outside his home. "What saved me was that I was a really good student," he observes. "That's always been my salvation—that, and I was good in sports. I didn't speak a word of English when I came, and in one year I not only learned the language but I was skipped two grades."

Not long after their arrival in the United States, Maria Bancroft gave birth to another son, a half brother about whom Petar says only, "I was the one who was supposed to be a failure, but it's my half brother who's shown the classic pattern of self-destruction and delinquency. He killed somebody when he was fifteen, and it was no accident. He's been married four times, and he's always in some kind of trouble. He's evading the law again now," he says disgustedly. He pauses, counting his thoughts and weighing his words, then muses, "Boy, life's funny, isn't it? My mother complained about my father's alcoholism, then married another alcoholic. She always said I was the one who'd come to no good, and it's her favorite baby whose life's a disaster.

"Wouldn't you think a mother would take some pride in a kid's success?" he asks, as if he still can't comprehend that his accomplishments meant nothing to her. "But it never made a difference, no matter how well I did; none of it mattered. When I'd bring home all A's, my mother would tell me I wasn't smart, I was just being arrogant. So mostly I was so lonely, I wanted to die."

The word *lonely* is repeated like a haunting refrain in Petar's life, the loneliness of a child who lived on the margins of family life—a child who was separated from a loved father first by divorce, then by death; a child who came to an alien world with no support; a child whose family moved so often he had little opportunity to become integrated into a community or life outside the home. "I was an army brat. We moved all the time—Texas, California, Nebraska, Guam. Those were the only good years, my teen years in Guam. I never felt like I belonged here, so I loved being outside of the country."

The years in Guam offered more than simple relief from his sense of being an alien on American soil. They were prized, too, because the community and the terrain provided seemingly unending opportunities for activities that kept him away from home. "It was a place where it was easy to stay out of the house, and there was a lot to do. They were glad to get rid of me, and I was glad not to have to be there. So I was always camping, hiking in the mountains, swimming, scuba diving, anything that kept me out and away from them."

Complicating Petar's childhood and adding to his other burdens was a birth defect that left his face somewhat deformed and disabled him from moving his head easily. "I was always made fun of because my face was crooked. I looked like Quasimodo. You know how cruel kids can be, how they pick on anyone who's different. So you can imagine what it was like to walk around like a freak.

"The worst part of it is that my mother always knew it could have been fixed easily when I was a kid. In Yugoslavia, when I was in first grade, the doctors told her that it was a simple surgical procedure to correct it, and that if it was done early, there'd be no disfiguration. But my mother would never sign the papers. I hated her for that, maybe more than for anything else.

"Later, when I was about fourteen, a teacher took me to a surgeon who said he'd do the surgery, but my mother wouldn't give her permission. She said God meant for me to suffer like that because the great sin of the Steprovices is that they're arrogant, and this would keep me humble."

It wasn't until he was seventeen years old that the problem finally was corrected. "By that time," Petar explains, "it was a much more complicated operation, so it was disfiguring and left major scars." He pulls down his collar and shows me the scar, then tears welling in his eyes, he says passionately, "I mean, I'm deformed and I didn't have to be.

"Every time I look in the mirror, I hate her. My face is still asymmetrical, and I'm very sensitive about it," he says, touching the right side of his face self-consciously, although I can see nothing amiss. "I feel very uncomfortable when I have to go up to the lecture platform. I compensate by being very clear, by being charming and making jokes. But that's the act on the outside; inside I feel self-conscious when I know people are looking at my face."

His words skid to an abrupt stop, his expression changes from one of anguished bewilderment to a pleased-with-himself smile. After a moment or two when he seems lost in pleasant thoughts, he continues, "I was just thinking about my two sons. It's always a funny feeling for me to look at them and see how beautiful they are. There's always this sense of, *How can this be; these two kids came out of me when I always thought I was so ugly?*"

Ironically, it was the military he hated that finally released him from the agony of his deformity. "I hated guns and war, but my mother insisted that I had to go to one of the military schools. Since I already knew I hated the army, I applied to Annapolis. I met all their requirements, but there was no way I could serve in the navy with my deformity. So Annapolis accepted me and then sent me to a navy hospital where they did the surgery.

"It was the one good thing that came out of that because I never wanted to go there. I had gotten a scholarship to MIT, but my mother kept saying that I couldn't count on keeping it and that they didn't have money for college without it." He sits up straighter, his lips widening in a smile that's more like a grimace, and says, "It's really grotesque. I actually found out later that my grandfather—my father's father, who was a famous musician and well-to-do—had left a substantial amount of money for my college education. But I never saw it; they used the money for a down payment on a house.

"So I was scared; suppose she was right and I couldn't keep my scholarship? What would happen to me then? The only positive reinforcement I ever got was at school, from my teachers. The house was dangerous; my mother and stepfather were always there to beat me up physically and psychologically. So school was my salvation, and I knew I had to get an education to get away."

Still, for a young man who was so marginal in the family, who had self-consciously *dis*identified with them and their beliefs so long ago, who hated his stepfather and the military life, his agreement to go to a military academy instead of MIT, even under the pressure he describes, seemed anomalous to me. He had, after all, flouted their authority many times before. Why, when the choice would determine the course of his life, did he suddenly become compliant? I ask the question; he remains silent, the conflicting feelings inside him evident in the changing expressions that play across his mobile face. Finally, sighing and shaking his head in wonderment at his own thoughts, he replies, "I don't know; maybe after everything that had gone on, I still had some crazy idea I could please her if I went to Annapolis."

Whatever his motives in going there, Petar's stay at Annapolis was to be short-lived. Although he was fourth in his class, he hated the authoritarian and violent culture and left at the end of his first year. "Those assholes were basically like my family—shouting and violent. So what was I doing there? To graduate into the navy so I could shout and be violent?"

His mother, who threatened to die of a heart attack if he left, continued to live but disowned him. "She completely cut me off. I was eighteen and absolutely, wholly, totally on my own. I don't remember ever being lonelier or more scared. I was one raw tear," he says, his eyes reddening at the memory.

Characteristically, he climbed over his fear and sadness, spent the summer flipping hamburgers at McDonald's, and sought advice from his English teacher at Annapolis, one of the several men who served as mentors or surrogates at various turning points in his life. "He told me I should apply to Yale, and he wrote a letter telling them about me and asking them to interview me. I thought it was a crazy idea. Even if they accepted me, how could I go? But I applied because he told me to and was stunned when they gave me a full scholarship."

He interrupts his narrative and shakes his head in wonder as he recalls that time. "All my life I've always found some man to be a mentor, someone who would be there to help me out when I needed it. I think that's because the image of my father as a kind, loving, and generous man was planted in me very early, and it's still central in my life. He was this real good thing who came from outside the home. So maybe that's why, as I grew up, I could believe there were some decent people in the world who would help you out and give you an even break when you needed it. Nothing in my life with my mother would have enabled me to believe in human decency."

And, indeed, Petar's life has been filled with men "from outside the home"—men whom he sought out and who "adopted" him, replaying for him the role of the good father he lost so long ago. These men not only nurtured, supported, and mentored Petar, their clear and unequivocal high regard also helped to affirm a positive sense of self that had been denied in the family since his father's death. "I understand; a mentor is like a parent substitute—a good parent—and there's no doubt that's what I've always been looking for," he remarks, his face a mask of anger and sorrow. He turns away, struggling to compose himself, and stares out the window with unseeing eyes. After a moment or two, he seems to shrug off his thoughts and turns back, "Maybe that's absurd at my age, I don't know. But wherever I've been, I've always had a mentor; I still do. There was this great professor at college; he's still my mentor to this day. The guy who introduced me to you is another one; he's from my graduate school days."

Despite the fact that he did extremely well academically and found a surrogate father at Yale, the triumph of being admitted to this prestigious university was soon muted by his complicated and ambivalent response to being there. For like so many others who have lived on the periphery of their families of origin, the sense of marginality remains long after it is no longer fully a reality. And always it is a double-edged sword.

The awareness of never fully belonging anywhere and the feelings of isolation that follow are not only hurtful reminders of the past but part of the loneliness of the present. But the very marginality that is the source of such distress also is a familiar companion, so much a part of the definition of self that it seems like the wellspring of creativity and accomplishment. Therefore, people may nurture their outsider status—albeit often unconsciously—even while wishing they could be rid of it.

These are feelings I know well. Some years ago, when I was invited to apply for a position at one of the nation's Ivy League universities, I was caught in just this mix of emotion. I was pleased and gratified to know that my work had been noticed and appreciated. But I was also anxious because being "in" was not only an alien experience but an unsettling one.

Just contemplating the possibility took me back to my childhood, to the moments when it seemed to me that to be a real part of my family I had to give up my soul. I knew once again the visceral fear of fitting in, the vague but powerful sense that to belong would be to lose myself. As I reflected upon the choice before me in adulthood, I felt the same conflict I had known as a child, the same conviction that I must choose between autonomy and belonging. I refused the invitation. To accept it was too profoundly at odds with my sense of self-in-the-world—a self whose intellectual and creative capacities seemed to me to be deeply linked to being an outsider.

So it was with Petar at Yale. He wanted to be there, wanted the status and success its degree promises. And although he was successful enough to attract the respect and attention of several of his world-famous professors, he could never give up his sense of marginality and allow himself to belong. "I hated it passionately. It was elitist and snobbish. I didn't fit and felt like I was second class the whole time I was there. My roommates were all from upper middle-class families with money and privilege, and I was this scholarship kid. Those American WASP types always make me uncomfortable. They think they're entitled to everything; they're arrogant, like the world owes them something."

The idea that someone could believe that "the world owes them something" is insupportable, not just to Petar but to all the others whose lives are chronicled in this book. For these are women and men whose sense of entitlement has been distinctly undernourished. They tend, therefore, to look with scorn at those who feel entitled to the goods of the world, seeing them as spoiled and self-centered. But while the disdain they express about the more privileged is deeply felt, it also allows them to hide from themselves their own feelings of anger and envy—anger that others wear their privilege so easily, envy of the sense of entitlement that they themselves can never feel.

Their mix of emotion notwithstanding, their lack of feelings of entitlement is also an element in their victory over the past. Most people who don't feel entitled to a fair share of the world's goods live with a sense of hopelessness that cripples their ability to go after what they want. But for transcenders, it's just another handicap to be overcome, another challenge to be met and mastered. Since they don't expect anything to be handed to them, they find their own way to get what they need.

It's this kind of self-reliance, this ability to organize themselves and their lives in their own behalf, that accounts for their success in the world. Moreover, since they expect so little, they tend to be grateful for whatever may be given—a quality that endears them to the people they meet and facilitates their adoptability.

His ambivalent feelings about Yale led Petar to chose a lower-profile university for his graduate studies. "I liked it a lot better," he says. "It was more comfortable, not all that old WASP money stuff that's such a part of those Ivy League schools. People there didn't think the world owed them anything; they knew they had to work for what they got."

His first job after receiving his doctorate was at a small midwestern college. There he met and married his first wife, Anne Marie, a young woman who sought refuge in marriage from her unstable and abusive home. But the *idea* of marriage was more compelling than the reality, and the two troubled young people quickly came to grief. "I hadn't worked out any of the stuff we're talking about now, and she had her own problems," says Petar. "But I was infatuated. She was pretty, and I wanted very much to have a family and be loved. I think I knew walking down the aisle that I was making a mistake."

But it was the kind of "knowing" that slipped away before it fully reached his consciousness, censored out because knowing threatened to deprive him of the loving acceptance he wanted so badly. To listen to his doubts, to allow himself to know them, to weigh them, was to inhibit action, forcing him to question his decision to marry and confronting him with the loss of a fantasy he wasn't prepared to abandon.

The experience of not knowing what we know is a common one, so common, in fact, that much of the work of psychotherapy is helping people to attend to that fleeting knowledge that lies right at the edge of consciousness. Somewhere inside an inner voice gives warning. We hear but we don't listen; we know but we don't allow ourselves to attend. So it was that Petar "knew."

It wasn't long, however, before his denial crumbled, and he was forced to know. Within months after the wedding, Anne Marie had an affair with another man. "When I found out she was unfaithful, I couldn't get over it," he says. Before the marriage was two years old, they were divorced. "After that," says Petar, "I decided I wasn't made for this family thing. I figured with my background I wouldn't be able to do it successfully, and I gave up hope of having love in my life."

Fleeting though his marriage was, its demise was painful for Petar. His wife's infidelity was hurtful, raising for him archaic fears that he wasn't likable or attractive enough to hold a woman. The loss of the home and family they made, even if only so briefly, heightened further the loneliness that had been his lifelong companion. His brave words about giving up the hope of marriage and family notwithstanding, the idea that he might be consigned to a life without love was frightening. In his usual style, however, he didn't allow himself to dwell on his fears. Instead, like all the transcenders in this book, he took the fall but didn't stay down.

Just as he had looked to school for reward and acceptance earlier in his life, he now turned to his work, producing enough books and articles to be noticed in the profession. Socially, too, his life was gratifying. He didn't have the wife and children he had dreamed of, but he had good friends, men and women who were his companions in the hours when he wasn't working.

Then a university in another state made him an offer he couldn't refuse. It was a move that would soon change the course of his life. For it was there that he met Adrienne Marshall, the woman to whom he has been married for the past five years. "I knew this was something special when I went to her house to meet her family for the first time and everyone said my name correctly. She had made them practice before I came so I'd feel welcome."

It was a pivotal moment for Petar. His name, which he had reclaimed in adulthood and which was so precious to him precisely because he had lost it for so many years, had also been a source of distress—setting him apart as an alien, provoking ridiculous mispronunciations on the American tongue. To hear his name spoken properly—to know that these people who welcomed him into their home had been willing to make that kind of effort in his behalf—was a rare and generous gift, a gift of acceptance he had never before experienced.

His guard fell; he was in love once again, not just with Adrienne but with her whole family. For here was the family he had longed for all his life—the family that would warm and comfort him, that would help to heal some of the hurts of the past. "My wife is an angel," he says with a broad smile. "This marriage is forever, believe me. She's beautiful and kind—everything a man could want. And she has this wonderful family; I feel about them like they're my own. I never knew people in a family could be so kind, loving, and generous.

"The last time I saw my mother was about four years ago, and I talk to her maybe once every few months. But I spend a lot of time with my wife's family. Her father and I do things like going fishing or to a ball game together—the kind of things every boy wants to do with his father but I couldn't.

"So I went from all the abnormality of my own family to this fantasy marriage and this fantasy family where people love and accept each other. My wife's parents really love our sons. They actually enjoy being with them, not like my grandparents treated me. And, believe me, my boys will never lack for a father. I'm with them all the time to make up for what I didn't have."

He pauses a moment, his head cocked, his eyes reflective. When he speaks again, his words come quickly, "I know, I know, it means I'm still being controlled by my childhood. But if it's to make sure my children have a better life, what's wrong with that?" he asks, not really needing an answer. For obviously, there's nothing wrong with his desire to give his children all that he didn't have. It's not only his children who benefit, however. In becoming the father he always wanted, he reassures himself about his capacities for love and nurturance and, in the process, takes another step toward healing his own internal scars.

"It's like a dream come true," he continues, his eyes shining, his smile bright. Then, as he hears his own words, he stops and corrects himself. "No," he says softly, "I didn't even have such dreams. I wouldn't have known what to dream for. It's not like a dream come true; it's like a movie come true."

For women and men who come from difficult and troubled families, a family that offers the succor they never had is a powerful magnet, drawing them in as if they had no will of their own. I remember well when, many years ago, I, too, married into a family that opened up for me a world of familial relationships I knew nothing about. My mother, always a difficult person, couldn't get along with my father's family. After he died, therefore, we were extruded from that large and boisterous tribe. Since all my mother's family had been left behind when she emigrated from Russia, she had no one here. Which left the three of us—my mother, my brother, and me—alone and beleaguered as we seemed always to be awaiting the next catastrophe that would befall us.

In my rational mind I know that, even in the Bronx, people in those years didn't barricade themselves behind the locks and bars that are so common now. Still, my internal imagery of that time is of the three of us hunkered down behind bolted doors from which my mother peered out suspiciously when some unlucky person dared to knock. Into that dark world, my husband's family came like a ray of light. Friends visited them and were welcomed warmly. Each Sunday my in-laws' sisters and brothers, together with their spouses and children, gathered to share the events of the week along with a meal.

They had conflicts from time to time, of course; they were, after all, a family. But no matter what their differences, their loyalty, devotion, and concern for each other never failed. For a nineteen-year-old who had never known a real family, it was like a miracle—a miracle made even more powerful by the loving acceptance with which they greeted my arrival into their circle.

That marriage ended after seventeen years—a divorce that would have come much sooner were it not for my attachment to my husband's family. Unfortunately, the collapse of my marriage brought my relationship with them to an end when my husband insisted that they demonstrate the kind of primitive loyalty that would exclude me. In what was characteristic behavior for both our families, my mother told him he was lucky to lose me and threatened to cast me out; his family closed ranks around him. The loss of those family relationships was difficult to bear, and I mourned them for a long time afterward. But the gift of their love and acceptance has remained with me for the rest of my life.

For Petar, too, the support and approval of his wife's family, and the sense of belonging he feels among them, has been a wondrous experience. In his professional life, however, he remains the consummate outsider, partly because academic disciplines define the boundaries of scholarly discourse so narrowly. When someone comes along with Petar's kind of broad and iconoclastic worldview and intelligence, it sends tremors of anxiety through the psyches of the disciplinary gatekeepers. Thus, although he's one of the most productive scholars in his department and gets the highest teaching evaluations, he's dismissed, he says indignantly, as "a mystic, not a real political scientist, because real political scientists do like they do."

Even if he wanted to, however, it would be nearly impossible for Petar to "do like they do." His lifetime of having to make his way as an outsider hasn't prepared him for the kind of conformity that's necessary to be on the inside. Instead, he's so accustomed to marching to his own drummer that he often has difficulty attending to the beat of the world around him. It seems natural to him to think what he calls "the big thoughts," to be more concerned with philosophical inquiry about what drives nations and people than with the narrower questions about political behavior that engage more traditional political scientists.

Still, while he defends his work passionately and is disdainful of the main current in his discipline, he's not without conflict about it. On the one hand, he's proud of his independence, of his refusal to bow to disciplinary canons for the sake of narrow career goals. But having in effect thumbed his nose at his colleagues, he's pained when they don't give him the approval and acceptance he craves. "They're busy polishing their buttons while the world's going to hell, and I'm writing books about the world going to hell and nobody's buying them," he complains caustically. Then, with a dismissive wave of his hand, he concludes, "That's the story of my life, isn't it, not fitting in. So what's the big deal?"

The attempt to shrug off his feelings, however, is belied by his melancholy tone and his body language, which tell a tale of dejection and rejection. So when I comment that it does, in fact, sound as if it's a "big deal" to him, his reply is etched in a kind of weary resignation. "Yes, it would really be nice, very nice, to fit in like in my wife's family. But I'm always a misfit, so I don't think I'll ever get that lucky, I mean, to fit into a department or a discipline."

The disintegration of what was formerly Yugoslavia has set him apart even further. As that nation broke into separate states and ethnic rivalries heated up, Slovenia, the region of Petar's birth and early childhood, commanded his attention with an urgency that surprised him. Without fully understanding why, he knew he had to go there to see for himself what was happening. So he applied for and won a Fulbright fellowship to study the rising conflict.

In 1992 the grown man returned to the country he had left when he was a small child—a country and a people with whom, despite his mother's attempts to wipe them out, he retained an emotional connection. This was the soil on which his ancestors had forged a life, the land that had nurtured his beloved father. As he wandered the cobbled streets of his childhood city, the sights, the sounds, the smells brought buried memories vividly to life—poignant memories of his father's love, cruel ones of the body lying rigid and blue on a slab in the morgue. There, too, he met people with whom he could reminisce about the past, women and men who knew his father and could fill in the fragments of picture and memory he had carried with him for so many years.

But his excursions into the past were soon brought to a halt by the exigencies of the present. Shortly after his arrival in Slovenia, the Serbs announced their policy of "ethnic cleansing," and the slaughter began. "It was a catastrophe. I saw Slovenian babies with their legs blown off, and the world just sat by and watched. Nobody did anything about it," exclaims Petar angrily. "Last time around—I mean the Holocaust—everybody said they didn't know. Now they know, and it's the same thing. So what does that mean? Probably that they didn't *want* to know then. And even if they did know, they still would have done nothing."

On his return to the United States, he found the media filled with sympathetic coverage about the plight of the Bosnians, while discussions about the other victims of Serbian aggression ranged from ambivalent to hostile. For many Americans, as for others in the Western world, the situation in Slovenia, which had been allied with Hitler's Germany during World War II, was seen at least partly as deserved retribution for past behavior. For Petar this was an intolerable reminder of his own past when his mother punished him for being his father's son. "People were holding the Slovenian people collectively guilty for their support of the Nazis in World War II, and it felt like this was the same thing my mother did to me—punishing me for being a Steprovic, for crimes I didn't commit.

"I felt wrongly sentenced and, when I read what people were writing about the Slovenians, I thought the country was being wrongly sentenced, too," he explains. "I mean, because people didn't like what their ancestors did in World War II, they didn't care that children were getting blown up."

Once again he was on the outside, trying to enlist support for his native land among people who still remembered the Slovenian betrayal of fifty years earlier. He spoke publicly wherever he could, wrote books about the war in the Balkans, and politicked—becoming for a while a mediator between the Slovenian and Israeli governments. "I thought that if Israel could come to terms with the past, then others could, too. I figured that just like my marriage is wiping out my past pain, a reconciliation between Slovenia and Israel would wipe out the pain of their past."

It isn't, he insists, that he's a Slovenian nationalist. In fact, the marginality that characterizes his life elsewhere makes itself felt among his

Slovenian countrymen as well. "I don't get along with many Slovenes. Basically, what I want is to see Slovenia and Israel make peace so that this ugly episode is put in the past, but many Slovenes—including a lot of the intellectuals—don't like what I'm doing," he explains.

Such declarations of purpose notwithstanding, there's something more than a political vision at stake in Petar's peacemaking ventures—something that rests in his past and generates a mix of feelings, both negative and positive. On the negative side is his revulsion with the kind of Christianity that is his heritage. What better way to make unquestionable and absolute his separation from his mother's fanatical Catholicism, and the anti-Semitism that accompanied it, than to take his place at the side of Jews?

On the positive side is his real connection with what he sees as the spirit of Judaism and with the Jewish men to whom he has turned for support and advice throughout his adult life. "All of my mentors have always been Jewish; I'm very comfortable among Jews. Before I got into all this stuff about the war, I spent my time studying dead Jewish thinkers.

"My latest mentor is Rabbi Frank Pearlman. I go to his Friday night services all the time, and I call him 'my rabbi' because that's what he really is to me, even though I'm not Jewish. He thinks I'm searching for an identity and that's why I'm always finding Jewish men to be close to. I have another Jewish friend who says I'm drawn to Jews because it's a mistake and I was really born Jewish," he says, his face alight with pleasure at the idea.

"Born Jewish"—a phrase Jews use to signify to an outsider that he's been fully accepted, that he's crossed the barrier that separates them from the rest of the world, that with him they can lay aside the uneasiness that, however slight, so often colors their relationships with non-Jews. Petar, of course, wasn't born Jewish. But the experiences of his early life paved the way for him to step into the Jewish world as if it were his own. Like him, Jews have always been a pariah people, vilified as apostates and cast out of the family of man. He's comfortable with Jews because he identifies with their pain—a pain he knows in the depth of his soul because it is also his own.

Moreover, there are principles in Judaism that exert a powerful gravitational pull for this man who has lived so long with so much rage. "It's the element of peacemaker that's embedded in Jewish life that I'm very drawn to," he says thoughtfully. "Even before I began to study Judaism, I always knew that Jews are called upon to make peace; it's a responsibility they bear. If you're a Jew, you can't turn down the opportunity for peace. I know no such imperative in Christianity.

"Recently my rabbi sent me some quotes from Jewish scriptures about peace, and there's one line in there I can't get out of my head: 'He who establishes peace between man and his fellow, between husband and wife, between two cities, two nations, two families or two governments, no harm should come to him.'

"I want to be that peacemaker," says Petar, his voice crackling with emotion. But it's not only a political peace he seeks; it's an internal one, a release from the anger that until now has dominated so much of his inner life. True, that anger has been an important element in his transcendence, goading him on each time he tripped and fell. But it also plays a part in his continuing marginality, in sustaining it even when it's no longer necessary. He understands that now as, for the first time, he relaxes into a life that brings him real joy, that fulfills his need for both love and work, and that, therefore, leaves him ready for an inner peace he's only just beginning to know.

four

Lynne Halsted:
A Reluctant Debutante

SHE'S FORTY-THREE, A DYNAMIC, SUCCESSFUL WOMAN, AND A PERFECT candidate for a study about people who triumph over their hurtful pasts. But she's also a child of the upper class, the daughter of one of America's wealthiest families, a child who never wanted for material luxuries, let alone the small comforts or basic necessities that so many others must struggle for. So when I asked Lynne Halsted if she'd allow me to tell her story, she demurred at first, saying, "But I've had such a privileged life. I grew up in a family where I never saw anyone look at a price tag."

I'd thought about that before I approached her, wondering whether it made sense to include someone who had grown up in the kind of wealth most of us don't even dream about. Like most people, I can't even imagine a life where you never worry about money, never think about what something costs, never know the fear of being old and poor. *Could a reader from a more ordinary class background respond empathically to Lynne's story?* I asked myself. *Could I?*

It was just this question, the idea that because of her wealth she had forfeited the right to a sympathetic hearing, that convinced me to include her story in this book. For this is the cross the children of the rich so often bear—the belief that their wealth nullifies their suffering, that they have no right to speak their grievances or to ask for sympathy.

Yet who among us is content to judge the quality of a life by money alone? Is the psychological fallout from neglect and abuse any different for the rich and the poor? Does wealth nurture the neglected child? Does it make her beatings any less painful? Does it make her mother's drunken stupor easier to abide? Does it make the loneliness of her childhood conviction that "the stork dropped me in the wrong family" any less palpable?

Yes, objectively it's undoubtedly better and safer to be abandoned in a thirty-six-room house with a half dozen servants, as Lynne was, than in a filthy apartment with little food and no adult in sight. But that doesn't mean that the privileged child doesn't suffer the costs of such parental desertion. For her, however, there's none of the sympathetic attention the poor child can command. Instead, we write off the trials of children like Lynne with a shrug and a disdainful comment about "poor little rich kids"—an attitude these children not only come to expect but adopt as their own as well.

The story of Lynne's childhood sounds like something out of an F. Scott Fitzgerald novel—a tale of incredible wealth, of lavish homes in a half dozen capitals and vacation meccas of the world, of narcissistic adults who roam the globe in endless pursuit of empty pleasures, of frightened and lonely children trapped in a golden cage. But ever mindful of the privilege her wealth confers—and persuaded that it mitigates her suffering—Lynne tells it in a careful, understated way, never dramatizing even the most explosive moments. Instead, except for momentary lapses, she remains emotionally contained throughout our hours together, often smiling when the subject would seem to call for tears, speaking quickly and fluently, her recollections dotted with reminders of her privilege, the words falling from her lips as if she wants to get them spoken and forgotten.

Lynne's parents were divorced when she was just past three years old. Her mother, who retained full custody of the children, was, says her daughter, "the quintessential absent parent, always very busy with her socializing, her charity affairs, and traveling around the world. Even when she was physically present, she wasn't really there. She was always involved with herself and the things she was doing. She's such an emotional stinge, I never could understand why she had children," Lynne concludes, her hot words giving the lie to her cool demeanor.

In some ways, however, her mother's absence was easier to tolerate than her cruel and critical presence. "At least the servants were always kind. But my mother's an alcoholic—the fourth generation of alcoholics in her family—with all the unpredictability that goes with that," explains Lynne, a look of revulsion momentarily erasing her smile. "There were many times when I'd wake up feeling smothered in the middle of the night and find my mother lying on top of me reeking from alcohol. She'd come in to check on me the way parents do, I guess, and passed out right there, right in my bed. To this day I hate the smell of alcohol."

She pauses, an involuntary shudder passing through her body, as she experiences once again the pain she felt then. "She was often out of control. You never knew what was going to happen or when she'd get mad and beat you up for reasons you couldn't understand. And some of those beatings were really memorable. When you're beaten at age three and a half and four by someone who's clearly out of control, it leaves an indelible mark. You don't forget the sight of the bruises on your body because they leave marks on your soul.

"I was very frightened of my mother throughout my childhood and always anxious about when the next attack would come," she continues. "I'll never forget the time she went absolutely wild because I hadn't memorized the Lord's Prayer to her satisfaction. I was a little kid, maybe four and a half or five, and I remember thinking *I can't believe I'm being punished for this.* Even then I understood that God wouldn't care if I didn't get all the words exactly right as long as he knew I was talking to him from my heart. I'm no longer physically afraid of her, but there's still an enormous emotional anxiety that remains when I think about those years," she acknowledges.

In a family where parents abuse their children, the children often act out their rage and helplessness on those around them who are weaker and more vulnerable. Thus, Lynne's brother became her tormentor, assaulting her whenever he got the chance—beating her up, tripping her on the stairs as she was climbing up, pushing her down when she was descending. As with all those who transcend their difficult pasts, however, Lynne Halsted refused to resign herself to being a helpless victim.

"My brother was bigger and stronger, so I couldn't win with him," Lynne recalls. "But when I was three and a half, someone gave me a life-size four-foot gorilla named Sam who became a very important figure in my life. For one thing, I could use him to get out some of my aggression that had no other channel. So just as I was tripped up and thrown down the stairs, I could trip Sam up and throw him down the stairs." For a child living in a violent and unpredictable environment, Sam the gorilla became the companion she could control, giving her at least some sense of efficacy in her world.

But Sam was more than a football to kick around. He was also her companion and confidant, the one she turned to for comfort and reassurance, the one to whom she could speak her inner thoughts. For Lynne was not just an abused child, she was also the marginal one. "I always felt like some kind of a space alien in my family. I never felt I belonged there from the time I was a very small child. When you've felt such a deep sense of being different so early on, an inner life develops at very young age. Sam helped me find my own way. My dialogues with him and with my inner self about being quite sure I was in the wrong place with the wrong family are very memorable to me."

She stops speaking, reflects upon her words as she shifts uncomfortably in her seat, then, fearing that she'll seem to be asking for sympathy, she reminds me once again about her life of privilege. "It's true that there was an enormous amount of parental neglect and that I felt totally unimportant and that no one cared about my existence. But it's also true that we were cared for well by a wonderful team of domestic helpers.

"In fact, my sanity today has to do, in great part, with Phoebe, who was the chief cook and bottle washer in the household and who was with me from the time I was born until she died a few years ago. She was responsible for managing the other staff and, of course, for taking care of my mother's needs, which kept her very busy. So her caregiving was of necessity extremely fragmented. Still, it was good to know I could go to Phoebe for protection from my brother and at least have someone who would console me, however briefly, when I needed help."

Where others may have had friends, neighbors, or relatives who offered some comfort, Lynne had Phoebe, the housekeeper, a paid member of the household staff. Did it make a difference in the child's experience? The question stops her, the easy flow of words momentarily suspended. When she speaks, she says uncertainly, "I'm not sure how to answer that. I certainly didn't think about what her role was when I ran to her for consolation. But, of course, I always knew she was part of the hired help. Those were very, very clear distinctions in my family."

When Lynne was six, her mother married Craig Halsted. Shortly thereafter, her father moved to Paris where he spent the rest of his life. "That felt like a terrible loss to me," she says. But while the loss of his physical presence was difficult, she would soon have an even more painful loss to mourn when she began to suspect that this man she thought of as her father might not be her biological parent. "For most of my life there's been this mystery about whether he really was my father," she says quietly.

"You know how children are about family secrets. I don't mean I actually knew. Obviously, I didn't want to *really* know. But I sensed that things were off, and I sort of vaguely knew there were other men in my mother's life. Later, when I thought about that, I began to put it together. There was one man in particular; he was considerably older than she was, and they saw each other every Thursday for years. It turns out that my brother and I may be the products of that liaison," she says, her words spoken evenly but her eyes betraying the bewilderment born of her doubt.

She pauses a moment, as if to let her mind catch up to her tongue, then continues, "When I was eighteen, my mother asked me to drive her up to visit this man—Frank Whaley—who was dying. At dinner with his family that evening, I sat next to his grandson who looks exactly like my brother. I was so surprised that I commented on it, but even before the words were fully out of my mouth, my mother was kicking me under the table. That's when I really began to understand. All of a sudden I remembered that I thought it was very odd when, on my brother's twenty-first birthday a few months earlier, this man gave him a ring with the Whaley family crest. So on the ride back to the city, I asked my mother if Mr. Whaley was my brother's father. And she said yes."

For Lynne, the news was, in some peculiar way, a relief. She and her brother had never gotten along. "He never got over being resentful that I was born," she says acidly. The idea that he wasn't really her brother, therefore, seemed to her to explain both his hostility and the fact that they were so different in interest and temperament. When she spoke these thoughts aloud, however, her mother insisted that she and her brother were indeed blood siblings. "But," says Lynne, her voice edged with barely controlled anger, "she said it in such a way as to leave me with a lot of doubts." Did it mean they were the children of her father, Charles Pardieu, or of this stranger, Frank Whaley? "She wouldn't clarify what she meant," concludes Lynne bitterly.

Searching for a way to still her doubts, she telephoned her brother.

"I told him about our visit with the Whaley family and that I'd found out we weren't really brother and sister. He said that I didn't know what I was talking about, that of course he was my brother, and that we were both Frank Whaley's children."

The idea, finally articulated and acknowledged, that she might not be the daughter of Charles Pardieu left Lynne feeling shaken, confused, and momentarily relieved. "It's all so typical of my family. There's all these secrets, and there's this culture where everyone acts as if everything is normal when, in fact, nothing is. So it was like opening the basement door and letting all the bugs crawl out. It was awful, but at least I knew what was behind the door."

But relief quickly gave way to anxiety. It was as if a key part of her identity had come into question. What did it mean about her heritage, about her sense of who she was, if her father wasn't actually her father? Like the adopted child who feels like a stranger in the adoptive family, she had clung to the belief that somewhere there was a family in which she would fit, that her father might be the loving parent she so desperately longed for. But what if he wasn't her *real* father? Who was she? And what was there to hope for?

It nagged at her like a sore tooth to which her tongue kept straying reflexively. Eventually, she screwed up her courage and asked Charles Pardieu if he knew who her biological father was. "He said he knew that my brother was not his child because he was conceived when my father was out of the country," she recalls. "But he believed I was his since he remembered the night I was conceived." She pauses as if to run the words back over in her mind, then offers up a small, wry smile, and says, "Not very convincing, is it?

"It's very disorienting, and even now I can't really put away the question very easily. But I don't think I'll ever know the truth. About a year ago I went to my mother and asked her about her love affair with Frank Whaley. I thought maybe if we could have a heart-to-heart, if I could speak to her on the level of passionate soul to passionate soul, she'd tell me. I've come to the conclusion that she doesn't know, so I suppose I have to let it go," she says doubtfully.

The union between her mother and stepfather, the inheritor of one of America's great nineteenth-century fortunes, increased the family's already considerable wealth enormously. From then until she was eighteen, when the marriage ended in an alcoholic and adulterous haze, the family's lifestyle became even more lavish than before. In addition to a half dozen homes, they had a helicopter, a plane, a Rolls-Royce and the chauffeur to go with it, and no less than sixty other people working to serve their every need.

For a child who already had far more material comforts than anyone needs, the marriage was a mixed blessing. On the positive side, it brought her a stepfather who, although physically absent much of the time, was a caring parent when present. "He was also an alcoholic but a quieter one and a sweet man, not violent and explosive like my mother," Lynne explains. "His youngest kid, my stepsister, was ten years older than I was and away at boarding school. So he hadn't been living with kids at home for six or seven years, and I think he was pleased to have a young child in his life."

As she talks about this relationship, Lynne's features soften into a warm smile. "I called him *poppy*. We had an affectionate, although nonverbal relationship. When I got older, I hated his politics because he was extremely racist and sexist. But as a father, he cared about me. We didn't spend much time together because they were gone so much, but when he was there, he was very generous in spirit. He adopted my brother and me when I was thirteen and set up the trusts for us. I feel indebted to him for his generosity."

His kindness, however, didn't extend to intervening in her mother's assaults. "He wouldn't get involved because he knew my mother's wrath. You have to understand, the whole environment was saturated with alcohol and violence. My earliest lesson was in how to mix drinks. They'd begin the day with Bloody Marys, then by midmorning they were drinking scotch. By noon they were drunk. They'd take a nap in the afternoon, then start again at four. And my mother was a very erratic and volatile drunk. So he was just as afraid of her as all the rest of us.

"She'd go out of control and they'd have these wild and violent fights—yelling and screaming, throwing glasses against the wall, turning over tables. Once we were out to dinner and, I don't remember why, but she suddenly stood up and turned the table over, right in the middle of this very nice restaurant."

The benefits of gaining a stepfather who cared about her notwithstanding, life became even lonelier and more chaotic than it had been before the marriage. "The family had all these houses, and I never knew when the next move would happen because we were always moving around from one to the other, depending on their whims or the season of the year," recalls Lynne. "But my parents were hardly ever there. We'd move, then most of the time they'd leave me while they went off to Florida or some other place, and I'd be living all alone in this house with thirty-six rooms and a staff of domestic workers.

"It was very lonely. My brother went away to boarding school when he was six, so he wasn't there. They didn't send me because, for some reason, it's not part of the tradition to send girls away so early. So I was really left all alone when my parents were gone. I mean there were the staff, who were perfectly nice, but it's not like having a family," she says, the word *family* filled with longing.

In her characteristic way, Lynne sought comfort where she could find it. Earlier there were Sam and Phoebe. Later there was the church to provide both a haven and a surrogate for the family that existed largely in name only. "My parents were too busy to go to church," she says, "so I was sent very early on their behalf. I'll always be grateful for that. The sense of isolation I felt and the feeling of being so alien facilitated a soulful journey for some power that would lift me out of that place. I found it in this small-town church where I went for a few years. Going there was like finding a room of my own, the first place where I felt at home, where I could hear myself and listen to my own inner life, and where I didn't feel unwelcome or threatened but instead was a valued member of the community. There was a kind of calm there that I knew nothing about before.

"It was relieving as a little kid to believe there was a relationship outside my relationships in the family that I could go to. When I prayed to 'Our Father,' I thought of it as having a dialogue with a father I could count on. I remember literally calling to God to get me out of that family. And I really had some belief that somehow He would guide me to safety. Later when I went to my first Adult Children of Alcoholics meeting and heard the phrase, 'There is a power greater than yourself,' I thought, *Yes, I knew that by the time I was six years old.*"

Once again, Lynne's concern that she might be seen as a poor little rich girl stops her. "I need to say," she insists, "that I could be hopeful and positive throughout all this because I was so lucky in so many aspects of my life. I lived in absolute safety; I never had to worry about living on the street as so many kids do today. I had everything I needed."

By "everything," she means material comforts. But the emotional nourishment that soothes the soul was almost wholly absent from her young life. Still, she maintains, there was something to be gained from the chaos and neglect. "Even though our household was crazy, there was quite a lot of freedom because there was so much neglect. So the neglect had it's positive side because that freedom taught me very early how to be enormously independent. And that has been one of the very important life skills that has helped me pick myself up many times and move on."

It wasn't her privileged life alone, however, that allowed Lynne to be "hopeful and positive," as the narratives of others in this book so aptly demonstrate. Rather, it's this kind of optimistic and positive reading of experience, this ability to extract something constructive from even the most negative ordeal, that is one of the core characteristics of people who transcend their pasts. Instead of feeling victimized by the circumstances of their lives, they try to learn something from them, to master them in some way that's useful.

I don't mean that transcenders are given to some Pollyannalike belief that there's a silver lining in every cloud. Or that they deny reality and refuse to acknowledge their victimization. Rather, they refuse to bow to it, to let it control their lives or the way they interpret and use the experience. This is a central feature of the quality we call *resilience*.

The Halsteds' restless migrations, as they followed their jet-set crowd from one party to the next, meant a procession of new schools and new friends for Lynne—a situation that heightened the child's sense of fragmentation and rootlessness. By the time she was in the fifth grade, she had attended schools in four different states, each move coming so quickly upon the heels of the last that she hardly had a chance to adjust before she was thrust into the next one.

In her usual way, however, she found ways to assuage her loneliness. "By the time I was ten and we moved to Minnesota, where I lived during the school year for a few years, I had gotten pretty good at making friends quickly. It was there that I began to attach myself to friends' families, and I saw that families actually sat down to dinner together and asked each other about what happened during the day. They even wanted to hear the answer," she says, the sense of wonderment she felt still alive as she recalls that time. "It was quite a revelation to find out that all households weren't centered on parental needs or how many tablecloths would be necessary for the next party."

When Lynne was about twelve, the mother of her closest friend, moved by the neglect she saw and by the child's obvious isolation, encouraged her to ask her parents to send her away to school. "She kept saying she thought it would be good for me to be in a place with caring adults and lots of other kids," Lynne recalls. Finally, when she was thirteen, her parents agreed.

For many children, being sent to boarding school is the ultimate rejection. These are the children who, no matter how difficult the family relationships are, continue to hope against hope that they can make it different, that if they can only be a little better, a little smarter, a little kinder, a little more loving, their parents will respond with the care and attention they long for.

Adults who have transcended their painful pasts, however, are those who understood very early that they alone couldn't fix their relationships with neglectful or abusing parents, that their only hope was to establish what Lynne calls "the right distance" between them-selves and their family and to find other sources of sustenance. "I think I understood when I was very, very young that I wasn't wholly responsible for all the bad things that were happening to me," says Lynne. "So even as a child I understood that I had to try to keep my distance if I was going to maintain my sanity."

Being sent to boarding school, therefore, was a relief, not a rejec-tion. It helped her to maintain the distance she knew she needed while it also provided the first supportive environment of her young life. For the first time ever Lynne could live in one place for a whole year among people who, she could believe, cared about her and wanted her there. "I was euphoric because life was no longer frag-mented. When you're a child and keep moving around like that, you never feel that you can put down roots anywhere. In boarding school, I was like a tree rooting itself. And I loved the community of women. I had never spent much time around women, and suddenly I was in a place where there were two hundred young women. It was a very powerful experience."

Academically, however, she didn't shine. "I wasn't a good student. I was slightly dyslexic, which wasn't identified and dealt with until my senior year. So, especially at the beginning, I felt like I was this slow, unattractive, worthless person academically. It was kind of an affirmation of the view of my brother and me at home."

He was "the Prince Charming," she says, the child who was defined as the smart one, the talented one, the one who would win the competitive sweepstakes they were set up for. "There was a lot of competition fostered between my brother and myself, and it was assumed that I'd lose. So when I didn't do so well academically at the beginning, it made me feel like the slow, dumb one all over again. It took a while to find myself and my strengths."

By the end of her sophomore year, those strengths began to make themselves known when, as she puts it, she "balanced out" her mediocre academic performance by excelling in social activities and athletics. "By the time I was in my junior year, I found I was a leader and could get people to collaborate on all kinds of projects and activities. That helped a lot. It was a chance to blossom, and I grabbed it."

For her family, however, she "blossomed" too much when she gained thirty pounds during her first three years at school. Her mother, as befits of woman of her class, is what Tom Wolfe has called a "social x-ray," a woman so thin she seems to have no corporeal substance. So when Lynne gained so much weight, her mother "completely freaked out" and forced her daughter onto a regimen of pills, diet, and daily weigh-ins at the school infirmary. None of it helped.

"It was a very painful battle," says Lynne. But while her words speak of pain and her grimace shouts distaste, her eyes gleam in triumph. For this was one of the few battles with her mother she ever won—a contest that continues into the present. Lynne Halsted remains a stout woman with the kind of good looks and disarming smile that inspire the regretful thought: *Such a pretty face. . . .*

For Lynne's mother, a daughter who was thirty pounds overweight would be a trial at any time. But given her expectation that her daughter would be presented to society in a great extravaganza, it was intolerable. "All my life I knew my mother had planned that I'd come out as a debutante and, as they say, be brought out into society. It meant nothing to me, but it was *very* important to her. And she wasn't about to present me to the world looking like that."

Her mother, never a graceful loser, would soon prove that she would spare no expense—material or emotional—to get her way. In the summer between Lynne's junior and senior years, therefore, she had Lynne admitted to a hospital where her diet would be completely controlled. "I was in the hospital for two months that summer and, of course, they were out of town the whole time," Lynne says, in one of the few moments when she allows herself to express her bitterness.

She acquiesced to the hospitalization, she explains, because she saw no way out. "I was miserable; I wanted attention; I guess maybe I even still wanted to please her. But most of all, I felt that I had no choice. I was still afraid of her; I had no independent source of money; I was a very naive kid who didn't know her way around the world. So I had no idea what else I could do."

Here again, Lynne's resilience—her capacity to extract something positive from the most difficult moments of her life—came to the fore. So although those months linger in consciousness like a raw and painful sore, she also insists that "it was a cathartic experience." In desperation to fill the endless empty hours, she began to read serious novels. "I read books like *Of Human Bondage,* books about other people's sufferings that helped me to understand my own and also to see how others coped. So in the end, it was a very important time for me."

Some time during that summer, Lynne's stepsister came to visit her in the hospital and angrily denounced the family. "She's ten years older than I am, and we'd never been close. So I was really surprised when she was so upset and angry about their putting me in the hospital. She told me that she had just gotten into therapy and had come to realize that we came from a very crazy family. She wanted me to know that and to know that help was available to me, too. It may not seem like much, but for me it was one of those defining moments in life.

"Obviously, I had some sense before that this family was crazy, but I could never allow myself to fully acknowledge it. She gave me the permission I needed to really know it, and it helped me to get away. A year and a half later I went into therapy and began the real process of healing."

Despite the nearly prisonlike surveillance, Lynne's weight loss didn't go according to her mother's plan. "She wanted me to lose at least twenty-five pounds. But after two months, when I had plateaued at twenty pounds for three weeks, I finally couldn't stand it anymore. So I fixed the scale to show I lost the twenty-five pounds and I got out.

"It was all to no avail anyway," says Lynne with a wry smile. "When I came out of the hospital, my mother took me to Europe to have the dress made for the coming-out party. But my debut wasn't for another six months, and within six weeks I had gained back all the weight I'd lost. So by the time the party came, they had to send a seamstress over to put a patch in the dress. My mother was fit to be tied, of course."

The debut and the preparations for it were pure misery for Lynne. As I listen to her describe the experience, I'm reminded of the way prized animals are displayed at a county fair, the difference being that the animal actually is valued. Lynne, however, was an overweight embarrassment. "I was being showcased, but I was never the daughter my mother wanted. I don't know; maybe nobody could have been. She's so narcissistic; she can only care about herself and what affects her. The whole thing didn't have anything to do with me, with who I was or what I wanted. It was her party, for her and about her. I was just the excuse. I was completely objectified, and I wasn't even an object they cared for," she says, her voice breaking ever so slightly, the words caught deep in her throat.

She stops speaking, looks away until she regains control, then, with a dismissive wave of her hand, says apologetically, "I know all this isn't the worst thing that can happen to someone. The whole business seems glamorous to a lot of people, I suppose. But it really can be a terrible experience—humiliating and alienating; at least that's the way it was for me."

College took Lynne another step away from her family, and she glows with pleasure as she recounts her years there. "I chose the college," she says, "because their application asked what I wanted out of my education there and how I would go about getting it. As a child, no one had ever asked me what I wanted or what I thought, so I was thrilled with the idea of being able to think about that and to design an educational program for myself.

"I blossomed there. It was a small women's college where the average class had eight students, and I needed that kind of small learning environment. Finally, I was being heard. It was as if I had found a voice," she concludes.

Finding a voice meant also beginning to deal more directly with her abusive past. Spurred by increasing reports of child abuse and by memories of her own battered childhood, she devoted part of her senior year at college to study and work in the area of child abuse. By the time she graduated, she had learned enough to get a job at the Child Abuse Council, where she was instrumental in developing a telephone hotline that became a model for others to follow.

As she speaks of that time, she leans forward, her shoulders hunched, her words gaining in intensity. "I spent hours on the phone listening to parents and children being able to voice what I had not been able to say as a child—their feelings of terror and their efforts at trying to resolve what was going on in the family. When I was on that phone with those parents, I was working out a dialogue I had never been able to have in my own family; it was the conversation with my mother I could never have.

"It was very powerful for me to see that conflict could be resolved differently from the way it worked in my family. It was also an extremely important step in the healing process for me. I was healing myself by helping others avoid the things that happened to me."

It was in this period that the form of Lynne's adult life, both personally and professionally, began to take shape. At twenty-two, she became sexually involved with a woman for the first time. "It wasn't a long relationship, and I went back to being with a man afterward. Then, after a couple of years, I said to myself, 'Maybe if I sleep for twenty-five years, like Rip Van Winkle, I'll wake up and find men as interesting as women.' So I've been a happily partnered lesbian since then.

"Don't misunderstand me," she warns. "It wasn't by some sort of psychological compulsion that I became a lesbian. I mean, I acknowledge my sincere interest in and passion for other women. But I also truly believe that I'm fully bisexual." She stops speaking, reflects upon her words for a moment, then resumes her effort at clarification. "The point is that I find that there are far more interesting women than men, many more women who are willing to do the psychological work necessary to enter into a really close peer relationship. So my commitment isn't to lesbianism, but to people who continue to work on themselves and with whom I can find that kind of sharing.

"I see some evidence that the men of my generation are trying to change, and that makes them more interesting. But most men have a long way to go," she declares. "So for now, at least, that means women."

Asked how her family responded to her coming out as a lesbian, she says with a dismissive shrug, "It never occurred to me to hide it from my mother or anyone else. I come from a family that didn't love or value its women, and I live in that kind of a society. So my mother's response was just what I would have expected. She assumed I'd outgrow it; she still does, I think. She's made it very clear that a woman isn't whole until she's had children and that parenting and child rearing are among the most magical experiences of life. To which I could only say, 'I'm glad you feel that way; it's too bad you didn't demonstrate it.' "

For Lynne, being a lesbian means being embedded in a web of relationships with women where she has found, in her words, "genuine acceptance" for the first time in her life. "I'm surrounded by a loving community, a community of women who have become the family I needed and never had." But such communities don't happen by accident. Or simply because they're made up of women who are also lesbians.

True, the oppression of lesbians, their sense of outsiderness, tends to bring them together in common cause. But for a real community to develop, a community of people bound together by emotional ties, something else is necessary. In the community Lynne speaks of, that "something else" is Lynne Halsted, whose energy and commitment has been the guiding force in building the community that surrounds her. It's part of the good works to which she has devoted her life—good works that, in this case, not only serve a larger social purpose but also have created the surrogate family that assuages the loneliness and isolation that dominated her earlier life.

Professionally, Lynne Halsted is, by anyone's definition, a success. Asked about her occupation, she replies, "feminist philanthropist." But, although she has indeed given away a fortune and continues to do so, she's not simply some Lady Bountiful engaged in the noble task of dispensing charity to the "unfortunates." Instead, she invests both her money and herself in projects that will make a difference, projects that have the potential to change lives and the institutions that constrain them.

In the two decades since she left college, she has been involved in over a thousand such ventures, bringing to them her energy and her considerable organizational and fund-raising skills, as well as her money. During this time, she has also been the spirit behind the development of two major philanthropic foundations and several other organizations, all of them devoted to a more just and equitable society.

She is currently the head of an organization she founded a dozen years ago, a resource center for women with wealth, "the only one in the world," she says proudly. Asked why most people would think such an organization is important, she replies emphatically, her words ringing with passionate commitment, "Because if the women with the greatest financial resources in this country aren't putting those resources to full use, aren't investing them in socially responsible ways, aren't starting small businesses, aren't redistributing that wealth through philanthropy, the larger society is impoverished.

"Money has been a man's world until the last twenty years. If we can empower women about money it can be as powerful a force as the vote was for my grandmother in the twenties and as driving cars was for women of the fifties. It's the last frontier, and women need to know how to make it and use it.

"Some years ago, when I was with a foundation that I helped to start, I'd watch women become silent and the men take over when the subject was money. And I thought: *What is this? Why am I sitting here quietly when I know as much as they do? How can I get these women—and myself—to start talking and take control when it comes to money?* That was the beginning. Now we work with thousands of women in programs that empower them and also that invite them to talk about money through the eye of considering their whole value system so that they can invest in socially responsible companies.

"We produce fifty financial educational programs a year for women, not just for the very rich but for any woman who has $25,000 of inherited wealth or discretionary funds. They're not just financial management programs either. They address money and family, money and power—the whole personal side of money and its meaning that no one ever talks about. What began as self-interest on my part—a wish to find a community where we could talk about these things—has become a national model."

In contrast to the rootless and peripatetic life of her childhood, Lynne has lived in the same house for twenty years and has worked in the same building—a women's building she helped found—for sixteen of those years. Her professional relationships are warm and deeply rooted. "I take great pride and comfort in having created a community within which I feel loved and valued. I've worked with many of the same people for at least ten years, and almost all of the staff of the organization have been with me for years."

As is often true with people who have been ill-treated in childhood, however, Lynne has had a hard time separating admiration from love. It's not easy for any of us, since the two are closely linked. Nevertheless, there are important distinctions between them. Admiration is connected to the public self, to what we do and how we do it. Love is related to the private self, to who we are, to what we can receive, as well as what we give.

For a person who has known the kind of cruel criticism that was Lynne's fate as a child, it's especially hard to grasp that difference. It seems instead that the only way to stop the criticism, to gain the love she yearns for, is to be perfect, to be sure she always gets it right. In the hands of a person as competent and talented as Lynne Halsted, a life devoted to "getting it right" wins plenty of admiration but is in serious jeopardy of losing out on love.

For a long time the admiration she won so easily felt to Lynne like love—a confusion that made for a long and difficult struggle for a fulfilling personal life. "As a child I didn't witness or experience intimacy anywhere in my life. So one very exciting and also very hard part of my adult life has been in learning how to be in an intimate relationship.

"Until about ten years ago I had fully internalized my mother's critical voice and believed if I spent more than an hour or two at a time with anybody, they'd discover that I was really a shallow and superficial person with nothing to contribute. So, of course, I kept a careful distance from people and didn't get into any long-term relationships. Instead, I was driven to build my sense of self through my work. I was so dependent on my work and my achievements there as a source of self-esteem that my life was way out of balance, not just my personal life, but my spiritual life, too."

For the past decade, however, Lynne has lived with her partner, Elizabeth, in a relationship that grows, changes, and sometimes falters as they struggle with the issues an intimate relationship raises for all of us. "Being with Elizabeth has been a profound breakthrough for me. It's the longest relationship I've ever had. Before this, I'd never been in one that lasted more than three years.

"We're very different, and those differences are beginning to cause strains," she says sadly. "Elizabeth is a person who has a very fear-based personality, and I'm one who has survived by denying fear and moving ahead. I see the possibility in things more often than not; she sees the pitfalls, the dangers. I know the problems denial can create, and maybe I've suffered because of it, but I prefer that as a defense system to fear any day. It's terrible to see the world through fear-filled eyes all the time."

She pauses a moment, looks away, then says, "Whatever our differences, I never lose sight of the fact that Elizabeth is a most unusual person. She sets the standard for what real love is because her love is wholly authentic, not rooted in the kind of narcissism and egotism that I saw so much of in my life. She's an extremely emotionally generous soul. I'd never before experienced anything like the quality of her attentiveness and her ability to listen and hear."

Her words catch her attention and momentarily stop her; then she continues with a shrug, "Well, maybe I never allowed myself to experience anything like it before. I didn't stay around long enough before this to allow it to happen. For me, the achievement has been being able to receive love and accepting that I deserve to be that important to someone. I've always done the giving part in relationships extremely well, but to learn how to do the receiving has been a major piece of work. And Elizabeth has been central to that learning. It's a great gift.

"So although it's not perfect, I've made real progress in my ability to be intimate. I came into my relationship with Elizabeth ten years ago at about a three on an intimacy scale of one to ten. Now I'm about a seven on that scale, and I'm thrilled to be able to say that."

She leans back in her chair with a satisfied smile, then, responding to some internal need to sum it all up, continues, "The most significant accomplishment of my life is having created a close group of friends whom I love and who love me. They're my chosen family. For the rest of my life I know I'll be in a close and caring community of people who are there for each other on a daily basis. My achievements at work are secondary compared to this one.

"Right now I feel like I'm in a major life transition. I feel very accomplished in my work: I've achieved many of the goals I set out to attain, and I'm also aware that my role is shifting. Elizabeth and I are in transition, too, and I don't know where that will end. So I feel somewhat disoriented at times, but I'm also very confident of my capacity to deal with the changes that are coming up. My childhood gave me a lot of lessons in being knocked down and getting up again. And that's given me a great capacity and confidence to deal with whatever I may have to face now because none of it will measure up to the difficulty of those childhood experiences."

Her family relationships remain distant. Craig Halsted, the stepfather who adopted her and with whom she maintained a warm connection after he divorced her mother, died fifteen years ago. At about the same time, she decided that she wanted to have a relationship with Charles Pardieu, the man she thought was her father when she was a child. But despite "a determined effort to try to get to know him," she says sorrowfully, "he died a few years ago without our having a very resolved or loving relationship."

Lynne and her brother have as little in common today as they did in their earlier years. Although they were both abused and neglected as children, he was the favored child, the smart one, the Prince Charming who was destined for success. She was "just a girl," nothing special, not worth much attention or concern. As is so often the case in such families, however, adulthood finds the siblings living scripts quite different from those that were written for them in childhood. She is the successful one, the child who got away. He remains stuck in the family pathology, a victim of his identification with his mother and her way of life. "My brother is caught in a very tight Oedipal relationship with my mother," observes Lynne caustically.

Like his mother, he has had a lifelong problem with alcohol, which he now battles, sometimes more successfully than others. "He got into recovery a few years ago and seemed happy in it. But when I saw him recently, he was very drunk. For awhile I had some hope for him, but now I begin to think that he's a lost cause again," Lynne says impatiently.

"My brother's professional life has also been a disaster. He's a deal guy, one of those people who's a lot of talk and no action and who's forever cooking up ideas that fall through. So it's been drama after drama. He's never held onto a job or really supported himself in his adult life. Every now and then he gets a job that pays really well, but he goes through the money in a few months."

Where Lynne has invested her inheritance wisely, her brother has squandered his. Where she has lived a socially responsible life, he has been driven by the same narcissistic quest for personal pleasure he saw in the family of his childhood. "He's gone through all the money he inherited and depends on my mother to bail him out. And she does," says Lynne, her words edged in disgust.

Her mother, who remarried again after a near-suicidal depression following her divorce, continues to live the same empty alcoholic and frenetic life that was the hallmark of Lynne's childhood. "It's a simpler life than she lived with my stepfather; they have three houses instead of six. But it's still a very upper-class, very lavish lifestyle. They're still jet-setters who go where the action is. And my mother is as busy as she always was.

"To this day I can go to her apartment and find her on two phones at once. I haven't had an uninterrupted conversation with her there in years and years. It always made me feel unwelcome to go there and watch her on the phones, so I've finally decided not to see her at home anymore. Now when I'm in the East, which is where she lives, and she's not traveling somewhere, I invite her to lunch or to do something else because if we're going to see each other, I want to at least try to make it quality time."

In the twenty years since Lynne has lived in California, her mother has visited her only twice. "She was very uncomfortable the two times she came here because she thinks I live in a hovel. In fact, it's really a very nice house; it's small but very comfortable. But it's not like anything she's ever been familiar with, and she simply can't understand why I would live this way."

She pauses a moment, then with a shrug and a knowing smile, remarks, "She writes rarely but she's consistent. The last note from her came after I saw her at a family party. She sent me the name of a new diet doctor."

five

Wayne Morgan:
The Rebellious Priest

I MET WAYNE MORGAN ABOUT TEN YEARS AGO WHEN HE WAS A recently ordained Catholic priest and was brought to dinner by a friend with whom he was having an affair. I was surprised then at the ease with which he entered our lives, surprised, too, at his openness in talking about the unorthodox situation in which he found himself.

Although we had never talked much about his history, I knew enough to know that he had taken some hard falls. So when I was thinking about this book, he came to mind as a likely candidate. But I hadn't seen him in many years, and I was uncertain how to approach him. *Why,* I kept wondering, *would a by now well-established priest risk the kind of revelations I was asking for?* The only way to find out, my friend who knew him well said as she handed me his telephone number, was to ask.

I suppose it should have seemed commonplace to me when he agreed without much ado to talk with me. I have been asking people to allow me to interview them for various books for more than twenty-five years, and only rarely does anyone refuse. Nevertheless, Wayne Morgan's easy acquiescence both surprised and concerned me. *Did he understand just how personal the interview would be? Did he realize that, no matter how hard I tried to obscure his identity, he might be recognizable to people in the church?* Finally, just before we were about to meet, I phoned him to make sure, "I want you to know that I'll be asking you to talk about very personal things, including your affair with Suzanne, and I'm not sure how effectively I can conceal your identity from people who know you." In his usual quiet way he replied, "I know. Let me know when you're coming, and I'll meet your plane."

Still, I was somewhat anxious when I arrived at the airport and looked around, wondering whether I'd recognize him after so many years, whether he might change his mind at the last minute. Perhaps he was equally anxious, I'm not sure. All I know is we missed each other at the gate. When I didn't see him there, I decided I must have misunderstood his instructions. *He's waiting at the baggage claim,* I told myself reassuringly as I set out in that direction. But he wasn't there either. I called the parish. "He's not in," a disembodied voice said. "Do you know if he's gone to the airport?" I asked. "He didn't say," she replied laconically. By then my anxiety had leaped from "somewhat" to "very." Just as I was about to take a taxi to my hotel, assuring myself that he'd figure out where I'd gone, I saw him sauntering toward me.

He's heavier now than when we met last, and his hair has grayed considerably. But he has the same puckish and irreverent sense of humor he had then, the same low-key surface that doesn't fully conceal the intensity underneath, and the same kind of philosophical and intellectual style I remember so well. So it seems fitting, when we finally sit down to talk, that one of his first references is a philosophical one. "I think it was Nietzsche who said, 'If you know the why you can bear the how.' I've always liked that saying, maybe because I've spent so much time trying to make sense of life."

The story of Wayne's life begins with his mother—a hostile, embittered woman who had little use for her only child. "She was a very angry, very unhappy person who was always looking for a fight. She stayed on top of me all the time. I don't mean she was interested in what I did; she wasn't. Definitely not. She just never stopped picking on me. It's not like we were having conflicts like kids and parents do. I wasn't fighting with her; she was just always screaming and hollering at me, like she just needed something to carry on about, and I was it."

Wayne's parents, Dorothy and Dan Morgan, were in their late thirties when they married, both for the first time. For six years, according to family lore, they had the perfect life. Then two things happened to mar Dorothy's happiness. She gave birth to her only child, and her husband had a heart attack. "For the whole first part of my life there was this worry about my father's health," recalls Wayne. "Then, when I was ten, he suddenly died. It was about four-thirty on a Sunday afternoon; we were watching a baseball game, and he went to the bathroom and dropped dead. Just like that, no warning, nothing."

Even before his father's death, it seemed to Wayne that he was nothing more than an unpleasant responsibility to his mother, like "a boarder in the house" for whom she was duty bound to perform some minimal service. "I always knew she didn't really want me around. Not that I was so perceptive," he adds with a harsh laugh. "It would have been pretty hard to miss it. She had no interest in me or my life, none whatsoever. I never saw a reaction of pride or pleasure in anything I did. She did her duty; she took care of my physical needs. But that was it. She basically didn't give a goddam about anything—what I did, what I thought—as long as I didn't cause her any trouble.

"My father is the only person she ever liked. According to her, the sixteen years they were married—particularly the six years before I was born and his first heart attack—were the only happy years of her life. When he was alive, I was in the way, like I was something that distracted her from him. I was an intruder in the house. After he died, it was clearer than ever that she would have preferred to do without me around," he concludes, his voice hardened by the anger with which he masks his pain.

The ability to use anger as a shield against pain is a common characteristic of people who transcend hurtful pasts. As with all such defenses, there are costs and benefits. On the positive side, anger is a mobilizing force, an often-empowering emotion that can help us to move beyond victimization and toward a greater sense of efficacy and control. It is, in addition, a way of managing the hurts, of containing them, of pushing them from the forefront of consciousness, so that they don't become overwhelming. The cost, however, is that years of translating pain into anger as a child can lead to the blunting of a full range of emotional responses as an adult. In Wayne's life, anger has been both a powerful energizing force and also one that, at various times, has limited the repertoire of emotional responses available to him.

Accordingly, there's a curious flatness when he speaks of his father's death. When I comment on his lack of affect, he replies almost listlessly, "I was upset, obviously. But it wasn't like we had rituals that we did together or anything like that. So it was more like the best thing about him was that he never got angry."

However he tries to explain it, it seems clear that his father simply was not a vivid presence in Wayne's inner life, partly, no doubt, because Dan Morgan's illness so dominated the family ethos that there was little else for his son to relate to and remember. "With him having a bad heart, what I remember most is there was always this thing where he couldn't exert himself; he couldn't do this; he couldn't do that."

Dan also became something of a phantom to Wayne because his mother jealously guarded her husband, claiming his time and attention so completely that there was little left for a child. "My mother was never happy except when she was with my father, and she really wanted him all to herself."

But Wayne's muted emotional response to his father's death is also connected to his anger, in this case, anger at his father because his illness left Dan unavailable, because he didn't protect Wayne from his mother's rage and rejection, because he died and left Wayne to cope with her alone. "With my mother so angry all the time, it was a relief to have him around. After he died, there was no one. He was the only one who could keep my mother moored down, too. So there was this ripple effect for me. Once he died, there was no controlling her at all.

"To this day, I can't understand why she had a kid," he says, throwing up his hands in a gesture of helpless incomprehension. "Maybe it was because my father wanted one, I don't know. Or maybe because my aunt couldn't have one. There was always this competition between them. It was terrible. My aunt was my grandmother's favorite, and my mother never forgave either one of them for that."

Despite the lifelong conflict between Dorothy, her widowed mother, and her older sister, the family shared a duplex—the two women living in the apartment upstairs; Dorothy, her husband, and son below. With Dan's death—the one person who could, in Wayne's words, keep his mother "moored"—the conflict with the upstairs family escalated into what seemed to the child to be "an endless fight."

From then until he left home, Wayne's life became a nightmarish tale of three women hooked together by their hatred—a grandmother who was as angry and unhappy as his mother, a spinster aunt who was totally dependent on her mother, and his own mother who hated them both. In the middle sat a small boy nobody wanted around—the victim of a mother who herself was an unwanted child.

Dorothy Morgan was the third and last child in a marriage destined for disaster. Her father was the son of a wealthy family; her mother was the pretty shop girl—a fairy-tale romance that turned into bad soap opera before the bubbles disappeared from the wedding champagne. Two children came quickly—first, a son; thirteen months later, a daughter. But their births only heightened the differences and escalated the conflicts between husband and wife. "My grandfather apparently was one of those high-spirited men given to grand gestures, and my grandmother didn't appreciate them. She was a woman totally devoid of any sense of humor. She always said he was a drunk. But I don't know," Wayne says, shaking his head doubtfully, "you can't believe their stories."

Whatever the truth of his grandmother's complaints, her anger at her husband and her disappointment in the marriage made itself felt into the third generation. In one last attempt to save their marriage, Wayne's grandparents decided to have another child. But as so many others before and since have regretfully found out, it didn't work. With Dorothy's birth, it became clear that there would be no savior in this marriage. Instead, she became the child who was destined to suffer the brunt of her mother's stormy discontent—an unloved child who would become an unloving mother. "My mother was supposed to be the reconciliation baby," Wayne explains. "But it didn't happen, and my grandmother never cared about her. It's like she couldn't forgive her for being born.

"There was always some kind of a fight going on between my mother and my aunt and grandmother. It was like they hated each other but were stuck together and couldn't get away. With my mother, you never knew when she'd go off. Sometimes just the sight of my grandmother and aunt was like a red flag to a bull. She'd go nuts and pick a fight as soon as she saw them.

"The line in the family was that my mother was always the difficult one. It's not hard to believe," he adds with a snort, "although they were all a little nuts. My aunt was a very odd woman, kind of crazy in a lot of ways. In fact, after my grandmother died, she went genuinely crazy; she really got very weird. My mother put her in a mental hospital where they gave her shock treatments. But she never was right again. My grandmother was okay; I think she liked me, and I got along with her. But I wouldn't say she was any fun," he says, grimacing at the idea of putting the words *grandmother* and *fun* in the same sentence.

For Dorothy, her husband's death was the final calamity. Unable to find consolation anywhere, she turned to alcohol. During the day she worked at a clerical job; at night she came home and got drunk. "She'd go to work, come home, drink, and pick a fight," is how her son describes his life with his mother. When his father was alive, there was at least something to distract her attention from Wayne. Now there was nothing but the whiskey to come between him and her rage. Sometimes the alcohol quieted her, but the moment was brief. More likely, it would trigger her anger by loosening whatever control she might have had when sober. "She was never a predictable person, but when she was drinking like that, she got even worse. You never knew what to expect."

Cooking, which had never been Dorothy's strong point even when her husband was alive, went wholly by the boards after his death. Wayne made do with TV dinners or whatever else he could find in the cupboard. "It was lonely as hell, but I was used to that," he says, his words etched in acid. "Besides, anything was better than having her notice me because that only led to her picking on me and more screaming."

His angry words notwithstanding, he was also frightened by his mother's swift deterioration. For it's quite possible for a child to hate a parent and still worry about losing her, as my own experience taught me long ago. I still remember the many nights, after my father died, when I stood at the subway station waiting anxiously for my mother to come home from work. I was seven or eight, old enough to know that her arrival wouldn't bring happy times, that I would more likely be greeted with a slap than with a smile; with an angry, "Why are you standing there like an orphan?" (a word she used often, as in "Other mothers send their orphan children to the orphanage, so you better behave") than with even a glimmer of understanding of the terror that brought me there. Yet as each train arrived with no sign of her, I became more and more agitated. *What if something happened to her? What would my brother and I do? Where would we go?*

For ten-year-old Wayne, the issues were the same. However cruel his mother may have been, she was the only parent he had. If she became unable to function, what would become of him? So while he was relieved when she hid behind her bedroom door and drank herself into a stupor, he also worried about the depth of her despair and kept trying to find ways to ease it. "As far as she was concerned, her life was over. She basically said that she wished she had gone with my father. I kept thinking maybe there was something I could do to make it better. But there was nothing I could ever say or do to please her," he says, his voice registering the same helplessness he felt then.

"I'd go into her room and ask her if she wanted to have some dinner, and there was no response; she wouldn't even answer me. She'd just sit there looking at nothing and keep on drinking. Sometimes when she came home with groceries, I'd look in the bag and if I found booze, I'd throw it away. But it didn't matter; she'd just go out and buy more," he concludes wearily.

Like the other men and women in this book, Wayne found consolation in activities outside the home. For him, these were school and sports, activities where he excelled, where he could ameliorate the sting of his mother's rejection, where his bruised sense of self could find some relief. But whatever solace he found in these endeavors, he remained the marginal one, the outsider, never fully belonging, even in those places and situations he sought out.

To protect himself at home, he spent his emotional energy tuning out—a capacity he developed with a good deal of success and that he can still call on in difficult situations today. But like all such defensive postures, this one, too, protects against one problem while leaving a person vulnerable to another. So while shutting himself off from the turmoil in the household was essential to Wayne's survival, he couldn't easily turn himself back on when the situation didn't warrant such vigilance.

From ten until seventeen, then, Wayne's life at home featured lonely meals in front of the television set and a drunken and abusive mother, whose fights with her own mother and sister provided the background music of the household. Then, after years of restraint, years when he endured his mother's abuse by turning a deaf ear, his own accumulated rage burst forth in a violent rush.

He had just started college when, he recalls with a shudder, "Something snapped in me. She started one of those arguments again. To this day I can't remember what it was about, but I knew I couldn't take it anymore. It was like a cold rage came over me. I didn't say a word. I just grabbed her by the throat and pushed her up against the wall and held her there so she couldn't talk. *All I wanted to do was shut her up,* " he says, his words hitting the air like fists, his eyes bright with the fury and the triumph of finally silencing her hated voice.

That was the last time Wayne lived under his mother's roof. A day or two later he moved into the dormitory at school and experienced the exhilaration of being freed from his mother's cruel presence. As he expanded into his new life, he met Diane Gardner, a nineteen-year-old sometime university student. "Diane was the only child of a pretty fancy family," he says. "Her father was a big-shot doctor who doted on her, but she had a very troubled relationship with her mother.

"She was gorgeous," he continues, a fond smile flitting across his face. "She was, well, not exactly aggressive, but a lot more than me. She was the extrovert; I was the introvert. She would talk; I would listen. We were a couple, but we weren't living together. I lived in the dorms; she was living at home, and we'd meet wherever we could. Then she got pregnant," he says, his voice rising as he remembers the shock he felt then. "When she told me, all I could say was a typical male response: 'How could you let this happen?' And she said, 'I did it on purpose.' To this day, I don't understand why, maybe just to piss her mother off even more."

It was a stunning blow. An abortion was out of the question, he says, "because she was going to have it whether I liked it or not." But the idea of becoming a father at twenty was more than he could fathom. He and Diane were little more than children themselves. How could they do it? What did they know about raising a child? How would they manage financially? Emotionally? His fears and objections cut no ice with Diane. "She wanted it and did it, but half of it was mine, so I had to be involved," he says.

Soon after Diane's announcement of her pregnancy, the young couple found an apartment and set up housekeeping. Wayne, who was by then about to enter his senior year at college, continued in school and worked part time, just as he had before. "We got along okay. Were we in love with each other? I don't think so. I mean, I liked her a hell of a lot, but love?" he says, his voice rising in a question mark. "I don't know if either one of us knew anything about love."

Although they were living together and expecting a child, marriage seemed an alien and impossible state to both of them. "We were sort of vaguely touching on whether we wanted to get married or not. We never got really into it, though, because that seemed more of a scary commitment than having a child. *I mean, we were only twenty years old.*"

With the baby's birth, however, all that changed. Suddenly, he wasn't "only twenty years old"; he was a father who fell in love with his daughter. "I didn't think I would, but I really liked being a father. Diane's mother wanted her to give the baby up for adoption. But I said, 'Over my dead body.' She was *mine.*"

For the first time in his life, Wayne had something that was his to keep. For the first time, there was someone who needed and wanted him, someone to whom he could speak and be heard. For the first time, there was someone he could love unequivocally, someone who would return that love and ease the misery and loneliness of a lifetime.

When he speaks about his daughter, his whole manner changes: His body language relaxes; his face softens; his eyes glow with love. "Her name was Erin," he says, a soft smile hovering around his lips;

his eyes distant as he seems to see the child once again. "Erin," he repeats as if to savor the sound. "She was a great kid."

Caring for Erin fell largely to her father. It was he who got up for her late-night and early-morning feedings, he who changed her diapers, he who fed and comforted her most of the time. "Diane liked to take the baby out and show her off, but she didn't much like the day-to-day stuff you have to do to care for a kid," he says without rancor. "I didn't mind; I really got into taking care of her. My big worry was that Diane might decide to leave, and I wouldn't have my daughter living with me."

Six months later Diane and Erin did leave, but not as Wayne had feared. Instead, they were killed in an automobile accident just a few blocks from their home. It's twenty-six years since then, but for Wayne Morgan the wound is still fresh. His daughter's death remains the central loss in his life. So his voice cracks and his eyes fill with tears as he recalls the moment when he heard the news. "A policeman came to the door, just like in the movies, and said, 'There's been an accident.' I went numb, like, this is somebody else's life; it can't be happening to me. All I wanted to do was close the door and say 'Go away and let's try this again with another script because this one's lousy.'"

His words come to a halt; he runs a hand through his hair and tries to lighten the sadness that fills the room. "There's got to be a better exit line than, 'I'm going to the store now,'" he quips, his lips forming a grotesque smile as he jabs at his eyes in a vain attempt to stem the tears. Then, after a struggle to regain control, he continues with a crisp, nearly mechanical recitation. "It was a Saturday morning, and Diane had to go to the store. She took Erin, put her in the car seat, and ran into a telephone pole with a little VW convertible bug. The pole fell on top of them, and they were killed instantly. No other car was involved. They said the street was wet and she must have skidded. But I don't know why it would have been wet; it wasn't raining."

With these words his control slips again, and he can't speak for a moment or two. Finally, his face etched in sorrow, he sighs deeply, then says softly, as if still trying to comprehend the incomprehensible, "It was only three blocks away."

The next several months of Wayne's life passed in a blur of pain and mourning. Alone and isolated, he had nowhere to turn. "I didn't have anyone I could talk to. Her father came over, but that wasn't any help. I don't know which was worse, being alone or having people around and feeling that they were staring at me. It was the same kind of feeling I had when my father died, everyone looking at me and not knowing what to say."

His mother, who had never met her granddaughter, neither attended the funeral nor tried to offer her son any comfort. "I didn't ask her to come," he explains. Then after a brief pause, he adds, "I didn't want to see her, so it didn't make any difference." But the bitterness of his tone belies the indifference of his words. For, of course, most mothers wouldn't have to be asked to console a child who has suffered such a tragedy. Nor would they have a six-month-old grandchild they had never bothered to meet. "It was no surprise," says Wayne. "She didn't want to have a son, so she sure as hell didn't care about having a granddaughter."

For a few months liquor became his companion and his solace. "I drank a lot during that time. It wasn't like I was out of control, like I had to have a drink. It was more like taking medicine, something to make me sleep. When I wasn't drinking, I couldn't get past the pain.

"When I drank, I could shut the nightmares out. Well, they weren't real nightmares. They were dreams about Erin and Diane. Later on I'd have these dreams where Erin was a child, not just a baby, and I could see her growing up. It was odd; they were nice dreams. Then in the dream, I'd realize this was a dream and it would never happen."

Sometimes anger would take over, offering momentary relief from his grief. "Once, about a month after they were killed, I went into one of those 7-11 stores, and there was a display of diapers right in front.

I took one look at them and went nuts. I couldn't stand seeing them; it was like I had to get them out of my sight. So I began to punch the boxes until I pushed the whole display down."

The accident that took Diane's and Erin's lives occurred in May, just before the end of the school year. But final exams wait for nothing, not even a personal tragedy of this magnitude. Two weeks later, therefore, Wayne sat for his exams and graduated from college on schedule. "I guess I had enough left to do it, but I still don't know how," he says, shaking his head in wonder.

Before their deaths, he had planned to go to law school. Afterward, he could find no meaning in anything. Law school, his future, even his life—none of it mattered anymore. "I didn't much care what I did and I couldn't think of anything else, so maybe three months later I joined the army and got sent to Vietnam. I think all I wanted was to find something that would make it stop hurting and someplace where I wouldn't have to think. That's certainly the army," he snickers sarcastically.

"I went to Vietnam not caring whether I lived or died. It was like, if I go, maybe some other poor sucker who's got something to live for won't have to. But I didn't die, maybe because once you get over there, you see that the object isn't to win the war. It becomes a kind of macabre game to stay alive. The object wasn't to take Hill 803 or some building they pointed you to. Maybe that was the goal in Washington or Saigon. Out there it was just to stay alive, and I did," he says, his bitter, angry words ricocheting around the room like bullets.

Asking a veteran of the Vietnam War to talk about the experience is asking him to speak about the unspeakable. "There's no way to describe it to someone who wasn't there," he says as he tries to find the words. "It was wet, *always wet*. The monsoons, the sweat—*wet*. You were never comfortable; you could never get dry. I have this image of this very wet country with hostile eyes staring at you all over the place."

As the memories wash over him, he shifts restlessly in his chair, his face contorted in pain. When he speaks, his words come out hard and bright, a barely controlled rage seething just below the surface. "Life? Life was below being cheap. It's indescribable. *They* weren't just the enemy; they weren't human to our guys, none of them; it didn't make any differences whether they were friends or foes. It was an impossible situation; anybody with half a brain could see that. Even the people who were on our side didn't like us. We burned their villages, shot their water buffalo, raped their women. And they were our allies." He hunches over, puts his head in his hands, and says through clenched teeth, "We didn't even bother to try to tell the difference between our friends and our enemies.

"I know, not everybody did that, but there was plenty of it. There was an incredible callousness and terrible, terrible cruelty. The war brutalized people so they did unimaginable things and didn't even think about it. The rules back home meant nothing. Over there they didn't exist; nothing you knew or understood before existed. It was a different time and a different place, a place no one had ever dreamed about.

"Even the worst movies, the most graphic ones, can't describe it. In the movies, you see people chopped up or shot up, but that was nothing compared to what it was really like. I couldn't even imagine before what could be done to a human body, how many ways there were to mutilate it. If you didn't narrow your vision down to staying alive and taking care of your immediate job, you'd go crazy. A lot of guys did, if not then, later."

The flood of tormented, angry words gives way to silence for several moments. Then more quietly, he says, "Nothing mattered when I went over there; I really didn't care about anything, not living or dying. It was like, if I'm dead, I'm dead; if I'm not, I'm not." He hesitates a moment, then continues somewhat awkwardly, "Then—I know this sounds a little weird, but it happened. I'd been there about nine months. We were at the base camp, and I was sitting by myself, propped up against the sandbags, and all of a sudden I felt. . . ." His voice drifts to a halt as he tries to find words to describe the event, and then continues, still uncertain, "Not exactly a sense of peace but. . . ." Again he stops, searching, and finally says, "It was more like I don't have to hurt anymore. It was like I did my penance in that damned war and now maybe I could do something with my life."

For Wayne Morgan, then, it was not just the real war he had been fighting but an internal one as well. Finally, he had suffered enough to expiate at least some of the guilt that had haunted his life—the guilt around his father's death and his anger about being left to cope with his mother alone; the guilt about hating his mother, about not being good enough or lovable enough to win her affection; the guilt about the death of his beloved daughter and the lovely young woman who was her mother. His Catholic soul demanded penance. By serving in Vietnam, he gave it its full measure. Only then was he ready to come back and take up his life.

But what kind of life would it be? It was impossible to return to the one he had left. Erin and Diane were gone and with them whatever worldly ambitions had driven him before. Now he needed to do something that would justify his survival when so many others around him had died, something with a larger purpose to which he could devote his life.

"I was twenty-six years old when I came back from that hell we call Vietnam. All I wanted was to find something to do that would give meaning to my life. But after Vietnam, how do you do that? If there ever was a meaningless situation, that was it. Meaningless, brutal, inhuman—there aren't any words. So what do you do? When all else fails, try God," he says with a grim smile.

Until his return from the war, religion wasn't a significant part of Wayne's emotional life. He had been raised in the Catholic church but, he says, "It didn't mean a lot; it was just what you did. I never said God didn't exist. It wasn't a question; I just didn't care. As far as I was concerned, being a Catholic was about obeying the rules. Basic Catholicism as it was taught then was based on fear. It meant you went to church on Sunday, put your money in the collection basket, and didn't screw around.

"I know now there's more to it than that, but that's what most people gleaned from being raised Catholic then. I went to confession once when I was a teenager and confessed that I'd gotten into a fight, and the priest yelled at me. I had enough of that at home with my mother, so I didn't go back for thirteen years."

But his quest for meaning and purpose brought him back to the church. "I had been brought up a Catholic; I was an altar boy; I'd been educated by Catholics. It was familiar; it made sense. So, like I said, when all else fails, give God a try."

His years of training for the priesthood, however, were not without conflict. At the beginning he was uncertain about whether he was making the right choice. When, in the novitiate phase, he was required to participate in a thirty-day silent retreat, he recalls, "Nothing happened to me for the first couple of weeks. I didn't have a clue how to pray. I'd never read the scriptures much either, and I was getting bored out of my skull."

Those were difficult days. He struggled with his boredom, probed his inner life for something to reassure him he was in the right place, castigated himself for not being able to "get with the program." Then, in one of the prescribed talks with the director, something clicked. "He referred to an image from the twelfth chapter of John's Gospel: 'Unless a grain of wheat falls into the ground and dies, it will not live.' That really struck home. The idea that you could give all of yourself over to something and out of that would come new life was very powerful. All of a sudden it made sense to me to live my life this way."

It's easy to see why the idea of death as the precursor of a new life was so appealing to Wayne. It not only gave meaning and purpose to the death and suffering of the past, it held the promise of peace in the future. But that new life would not be easy to come by.

Two years later, at the end of the novitiate, he took his first vows and embarked on the next step on the long road to the priesthood. But now a new set of doubts emerged, as it became increasingly clear that the self-reliance that was so necessary to his survival earlier in his life was a handicap in a community of brothers under God.

The question was no longer whether he *wanted* to be a priest but whether he *could* be, whether he could find a way to accommodate to the life and discipline of the order and to fit in with his peers. "I enjoyed the work when I was in the seminary—teaching, studying. It was meaningful and productive. But I didn't get along well in the community," he says with an impatient shrug.

A lifetime of standing on the outside left him unprepared for being on the inside. And his questioning, iconoclastic style was certainly not destined to make friends in a setting where conformity was prized. "I'm not now and wasn't then a particularly pious person, at least not in that outward, ritualistic kind of piety that's expected. And I wasn't real great at following orders, either. The first vows you take are to poverty, chastity, and obedience. I've always been good at poverty, but the other two, well, that's something else," he says with a wry smile.

He was the oddball in the group, the misfit, just as he had been in his family. "It felt like a replay of my whole life. I was always doing something wrong." Feeling left out, as if once again there was no place where he could find acceptance, he retreated into himself and became increasingly isolated from those around him. In such an emotional setting, it became nearly impossible for him to submit blindly to the discipline of superiors—or to the God he still wasn't sure existed. "I wasn't sure how much God came into it for me at that time. I still had to figure all that out and find a way to reconcile Christianity with some of the things I saw around me. Later, when I went to do my graduate study in theology, I learned to think about God in different ways."

But while his graduate studies engaged him deeply, his relationships with others remained difficult, and criticism swirled around him. In his third year, therefore, the director of his program told him that there was some concern about whether he was "psychologically suited" for the priesthood. For Wayne, who thought he finally was doing well, it seemed to affirm his lifelong belief that "good things always come to an end."

He began to question himself. "I felt like they were saying we don't like you as a person; your whole personality isn't acceptable, and you're just not good enough. I began to think maybe they knew more than I did; maybe I didn't belong there. The really major commitment I had to make—being ordained—was coming up in a year, and I thought, *I don't want to live with a lot of people who don't want me.* I'd already lived that scene with my mother."

In his characteristic fashion, he covered over his pain with anger. "I was really pissed at them for getting on my case," he recalls. But his anger couldn't fully protect him from feeling hurt and bewildered. *What had gone wrong? How could this happen when he thought he was doing so well?* Finally, with no answers to his questions and feeling increasingly rejected and abandoned, he sought comfort in the arms of a woman, breaking his celibacy vows for the first but not the last time. "I had this affair with—call her Joan—if you can say two unmarried people are having an affair. We probably went to bed three times, then she decided she didn't want to be involved, and it ended."

He looks away, agitated, and has trouble keeping his voice steady as the memory of the painful feelings of that turbulent time sweeps over him again. It wasn't the loss of Joan herself that was so difficult. Rather, it was another rejection in a life already too full of them that was so hard to bear. For no matter how often we experience it, we never get used to rejection. Instead, as each one piles on top of the others, the burden can become nearly unbearable. "I felt so bad, I think I went a little nuts. It wasn't her so much. I felt like I'd never be able to make a go of anything, so what good was I? What good was my life? I became deeply depressed, nearly suicidal, and that's when I went into therapy.

"I was scared, too. I thought they'd certainly throw me out after that mess. And after coming that far, I really wanted to go on. So I went to the director and threw myself on his mercy. Since I was getting help, he agreed to let me stay."

A year later Wayne was ordained, after which he completed his last year at the theological seminary. His work—whether student or priest—went well as always. But his troubles weren't over. "I still felt out of place in the community. I didn't fit in, and I kept thinking it wasn't going to work out well."

As his feelings of loneliness and isolation escalated, so did his doubts. Would he ever fit anywhere? Would they decide that he wasn't suited for the life he had chosen? As if to provoke the gods and confirm their judgment, he turned once again to a woman.

He met Suzanne when they were both working the night shift on a crisis hotline. It's stressful work, listening to the desperate night after night, trying to comfort them, to give them some reason to stay alive for one more hour, one more day. It's like being in a war, only this time the object is life, not death. And like those on the front lines of any war, the women and men who do this work tend to form bonds of compassion and understanding to help them through the long and trying nights.

"At first we'd be in touch periodically when we weren't working, just hello and how are you kind of stuff," recalls Wayne. "After a while, we got to be friends. One night we went out to dinner, and afterward we went back to her apartment and went to bed. We didn't plan it; it just happened.

"It was weird; I kept thinking, *Why am I here?* But the truth is, I knew why I was there. I felt good about the work, but my relationships in the community weren't good at all. I was surrounded by people, yet I was alone. I wanted to be close to somebody. I wanted somebody to be my friend."

Suzanne soon became more than a friend, and it wasn't long before they were seeing each other regularly. Meanwhile, he graduated from the seminary and was assigned to a parish in a city about a hundred miles away. For the first time since he'd entered training, he seemed to have found a home. "I wanted something where I'd be dealing with the sacraments, and I got it. It was a good place with a pretty good group of guys. We weren't the closest, but there were no open antagonisms. People got along, and I fit in a lot better than I ever had. I really enjoyed the work. I found that I was very good at preaching; people enjoyed the sermons and homilies. I wasn't floundering around anymore; I had a pretty clear vision of what I wanted to do and what I was about."

Once a week on his day off, he drove the hundred miles to see Suzanne. "In one sense it was the perfect relationship for me. I enjoyed what I was doing at work, and I had somebody who liked me and was happy to have me come and spend the night."

He speaks the words lightly, but, in fact, the relationship was so appealing to Wayne because it was more than just a place to "spend the night." He was a man starved for affection, and Suzanne gave it in abundance. He was a man who had never been loved, and she loved him. He was a man who had never known acceptance and approval, and she offered it. In that atmosphere, his emotional side—his ability to relate intimately, to permit vulnerability—which had been kept under protective wraps for so long, came out of hiding. Socially, too, Suzanne opened a world he hadn't known before. "We could go to a nice restaurant and have dinner. It was like being a normal person, going out on a date. I'd never been out on a date before," he says, his eyes gleaming with the delight of having been able to do so.

Finally, he felt normal—a man who had love and work and found satisfaction in both. He was wholly unconflicted about breaking the celibacy vow. "To be honest with you, I had no conflict about what I was doing. I can understand the idea of celibacy and that it might make it more difficult to do the work if you have a wife and children. It makes a certain amount of sense that you should devote yourself wholly to the work. But to me it wasn't essential to what I was about or what I was trying to do.

"What I believe is that, in most things, people do the best they can. I was doing the best I could, so I wasn't going home and whipping myself about doing something bad. Besides," he adds with an impish grin, "I was great at living up to poverty and getting better at obedience."

This was, for Wayne, a nearly idyllic time, a period when he had everything he wanted. True, as they became closer and he and Suzanne began to talk about the future, he was conflicted about the choice he might be called upon to make. The thought of giving up either his work or his love, and the new life she had opened up for him, filled him with a terrible sadness. But the question of their future didn't loom large enough to diminish his pleasure in the present. Rather, it was renewed trouble at work that set in motion a chain of events that would throw his life up in the air again.

"Nothing's ever perfect," he says with a weary sigh. "I suppose it would have had to come to a head anyway, but it all escalated when they changed pastors in the parish I was in. They brought in a new guy who was a very rigid and stupid man. There aren't many dumb people in my order, but he was one of them. A dumb man in a position of authority—that's a bad combination."

After several months of conflict, the situation became intolerable, and Wayne applied for a leave. "I said, 'I don't need this in my life,' so I took a leave of absence, picked up the phone and called Suzanne, and said, 'I'm moving in.' "

Officially, his superiors in the order didn't know he was living with a woman. Unofficially, explains Wayne, "They probably surmised what was going on, but they don't pry into your life. If you're out, you're out. Then, after a year, you have to make a decision—back in, or out for good."

The year with Suzanne was rife with conflict and turmoil. He was thirty-eight years old and had spent a decade readying himself for the priesthood. He loved being a priest. It was useful and productive work, and he was good at it. When he thought about giving it up, he became depressed. If not that, what else would he do? How would he live? What would engage him? What would give meaning and purpose to his life?

Although life with Suzanne could be deeply gratifying, there were problems there as well. It was hard for her to live with his episodic bouts of doubt and depression. Her idea of an intimate relationship was quite different from his—a common difficulty in relations between women and men these days. "We really cared about each other. But after a while I couldn't really visualize being able to sustain the relationship, partly because of who I am and partly because of who she is.

"I thought ultimately I wouldn't be able to give her what she wanted, emotionally and psychologically. I think I have more tolerance for processing the kind of emotional stuff she wanted to talk about and deal with than a lot of people. But it didn't seem like it was enough for her."

His doubts and fears notwithstanding, as the moment of decision approached, he asked her to marry him. It's unclear what he would have done had she accepted, but he wasn't put to the test. She refused, partly because she understood how deep his ambivalence went, and partly because she had her own doubts about their prospects for a long-term future together. "It was a mixed thing when she said no," he says, pausing a moment to order his thoughts. "But mostly I think I was relieved."

It has been nearly ten years since their romantic relationship ended, but Wayne and Suzanne remain close friends. They speak almost weekly and visit when they can, often spending his vacation together in the city where she lives. "I stay with Suzanne when I come to town. We get along fine; she enjoys having me around, and I enjoy being there.

But after I went back in the order, there was never any attempt, or even desire, to turn it into anything but a very good friendship."

Asked whether he can imagine breaking his vow of celibacy again, he thinks a long while, then says somewhat doubtfully, "I suppose. But that's not really the point. These panels on celibacy always end up talking about sex as opposed to intimacy. I don't see myself getting horny one night and going out to find someone in a bar.

"If you're asking whether there have been women I've been attracted to, the answer is yeah, sure. But it's not what I'm about. I don't want to hurt anybody, and if I got into a relationship with a woman, it wouldn't end well. Not just because I'm a priest either, but because I don't think I could live in an intimate relationship for any length of time."

Listening to these words it's easy to conclude that he escaped into the priesthood because he's too frightened to risk the demand, the drama, and the vulnerability an intimate relationship requires. But it's too simple an explanation for a complex man with a complicated history behind him. The death of his father, the rejection by his mother, a boyhood surrounded by three troubled and rageful women, the loss of his adored infant daughter, the devastating experience of Vietnam—all these went into the making of a priest. True, his doubts about his ability to sustain an intimate relationship probably also are related to his choice of a profession. But they're only one element in that choice, one he may not have acted on if all the others had not come together to give him such a powerful push.

Today, Wayne Morgan is at peace with his life and his chosen profession. "I make meaning out of my life by relatively small things— trying to be kind to people; facilitating their relationship with the church, and, hopefully, thus with God; being there when people need me. I have an ability to talk honestly with people and not put obstacles in their way. When someone comes to me for help, I don't judge or condemn them. I try to make it easier for them to do what they want with their lives.

"In the gospel reading today Jesus was speaking to Nicodemus and said, 'I have not come to condemn the world but to save it.' Not that I think I'm going to save the world, but most people have a very difficult time living. It's hard to do. And if I can make it a little more livable for them, then my life has meaning."

About his relationship to God, he now says, "I like God. I can pray; I feel His presence in my life; He's someone I can talk to so I don't feel alone. But part of it is always a mystery. Is God omnipotent? I don't know. But I do know He's not some kind of a bookkeeper up there counting up the good and the bad things we do. I think God wants people to do the best they can, and if they've done that and acted in good faith, that's fine with Him."

His interpersonal relationships with both peers and supervisors have improved substantially over the years. But he remains at the edge of community life, not necessarily because others keep him there now, but because it's where he's most comfortable. For when, as a small child, he accepted his marginality in the family, it became part of who he is, how he experiences himself in the world, and how he orients to it.

"I'm about as marginal as a member of this order can get," he says. "My relationships are okay; they're a lot better than they were. But I think I'm always going to feel like an outsider; I'll never be fully one of them. That's okay, though. It's where I've been all my life, and you get so used to something you can live with it comfortably most of the time."

Like the others in this book for whom marginality is a way of life, Wayne sees benefits as well as costs. It may have hindered his ability to belong anywhere, he says, but it has also given him a "sense of freedom"—freedom to think, to be—that he values deeply. "I don't identify myself totally with a certain group or a certain way of doing things, not even the order. I mean at some level I do; I identify with a lot of the good in it. But I don't spout the party line."

Finally, then, Wayne Morgan remains a maverick, an irreverent priest with a puckish sense of humor, his own vision, and his own version of what it means to be a religious man and to serve God. "I guess," he says, rubbing his chin ruefully, "I've never quite gotten the vocabulary down right." And it's not likely that he ever will.

six

Ana Guttierez: From Migrant Farmworker to Ph.D.

I HEARD ABOUT ANA GUTTIEREZ FROM A CLOSE FRIEND WHO WAS, AT the time, Ana's professor and mentor. "She's a remarkable young woman, perfect for your study," my friend assured me as she sketched the details of Ana's past. So I knew before we met that she was the child of migrant farmworkers who had spent most of her life following the crops in California's Imperial Valley and now, at thirty-three, was completing a master's degree in psychology.

Having lived in California most of my adult life, I've driven through the Imperial Valley many times, marveling at the richness of the seemingly endless miles of farmland in this region that's often called the nation's market basket. Each time I see the farmworkers bending low over the crops, their skin lined and darkened by years of working in the hot western sun, I find myself reflecting on the extremes of wealth and poverty this valley knows. The small farmers who once struggled to scrape a meager living out of the soil are long gone, replaced by big growers—sometimes by agribusiness, large corporations owning huge properties that are professionally managed, sometimes by very large extended-family farms that are owner operated. Therefore, the valley today is a land where generally those who own the soil live in abundance while those who work it exist in poverty and degradation few of us can imagine.

What my eyes have seen has been reinforced by what I've read about the deplorable conditions under which California's migrant farmworkers live and work. Long before I met Ana Guttierez, therefore, I knew that small children usually work the fields with their parents; that schooling can be hit or miss; that the struggle for daily existence, the need to move on to the next crop, often takes precedence over such concerns as whether children learn English, know how to read, or can do their sums. So as I listened to my friend sing Ana's praises, I kept wondering, *How does a person get from there to here?* Indeed, given the isolated, impoverished, and backbreaking life that is the farmworker's lot, it seemed remarkable that this young woman even knew there was a "here" here.

Now, as I climb the steps to her apartment on a hot summer day, I see her standing in the doorway, a welcoming smile lighting her lovely dark eyes. *Nobody told me she's so beautiful,* I think, as I take in her sensuously ripe figure encircled by a form-fitting sundress, the thick mass of wavy brown-black hair cascading down her bare shoulders, the silken smooth olive-toned skin stretched over a high-cheekboned face innocent of makeup.

While my mind struggles to integrate this unexpected vision, Ana and I exchange greetings a bit awkwardly, both of us aware that I, a total stranger, am about to invade the most private domains of her life. Then she leads me into the small, cramped apartment and introduces me to her partner, Russell Sawyer; his five-year-old daughter, Erica, who lives with them part time; and their eight-month-old son, Douglas. Another daughter, thirteen-year-old Angela, the child of

Ana's first marriage, is visiting her father who still lives in California's agricultural heartland.

Russell, she explains, is taking Erica and Douglas out for the afternoon so we can talk privately. But the children don't cooperate easily. Erica is absorbed in her game and wants to finish it; Douglas is tired and resists getting his diaper changed. It's a scene that would raise the temperature in most families. But Ana calmly lends Russell a hand in assembling the children and preparing them to leave.

When they're gone, she leans back on the couch for a moment, as if to gather her strength for what lies ahead, then says, "I've been thinking about what we'd talk about, and I keep wishing I had more happy memories to tell you." But happy memories are in short supply for those who grow up in migrant-labor camps, where the workday begins at dawn and ends at dark, where the hours in between are spent in backbreaking labor in the fields, where home is a tiny one-room shack without heat or running water, and where each day parents manage to put food on the table for their children is a victory against overwhelming odds.

Like so many other young Mexicans, Ana's parents, Carlos Delgado and Yolanda Rivera, walked across the border to join the legion of illegal aliens who work the fields and clean the houses in states like California, Texas, Arizona, and New Mexico. They didn't know each other then, but they were lured by the promise of a life that was more than they could expect in their native land.

Carlos went to work in the fields; Yolanda cleaned houses and took care of other people's children. Like all illegals, they spent a lot of time looking over their shoulder. For although illegal immigration has always been fostered by large growers looking for cheap and easily exploitable labor, the idea was to allow the immigrants in when they were needed and to send them back home when the job was done. The illegals, therefore, never knew when a sudden raid by the immigration police would end in their deportation. Consequently, the community of illegals has always been governed by caution and bound by fear of disclosure.

This was the world Carlos and Yolanda entered, an isolated world where social life generally was confined to others like themselves. It wasn't long before they met and decided to marry. As illegals, however, they couldn't risk a marriage in the United States. So they returned to the village in Mexico where Yolanda's parents lived, celebrated their marriage surrounded by her family, and shortly afterward walked back across the border to begin the life they would live from then on.

Now, as she speaks of that life, their daughter describes the mean and degraded conditions that defined their existence. "My parents didn't become legals—permanent residents—until after we were born. Then sometime after we were older, they actually became citizens. It didn't really make a difference in how we lived.

"As agricultural workers, we lived mostly on the farmers' land in the housing they provided. If you haven't seen it, it's pretty hard to imagine. There's row upon row of these little shacks that are probably smaller than this living room," she explains, her eyes sweeping across the small, cramped room in which we're sitting. "Everybody is crowded together, living on top of each other. And, of course, there's no plumbing or running water. We used outhouses.

"I've forgotten a lot of my early childhood. But the outhouses are etched in my memory because I was so scared to look down in them. You'd see awful things floating in there. I remember one time I looked down and saw a dead cat. When I think about it now, I can still remember the terror I felt," she says with a shudder.

Life for the Delgados was dictated by the crops, which meant that where they lived and for how long depended on what crop was ready for harvest that week or month. Most of their moves took them to a shack on a farmer's land that was no different from the one they left. "You never had the feeling that anyplace was home," says Ana as she speaks of the rootlessness that was the hallmark of her childhood.

Once, in what seemed to the family a stroke of extraordinary good luck, they were able to move out of the camps and into a place of their own. It, too, was little more than a shack, one that had years of filth oozing from every plank of wood in the walls. But for Ana, who was four years old at the time, it was home. "When we first got it, it was disgustingly dirty, feces smeared all over the walls, piles of filth and litter and junk strewn around everywhere. It wasn't fit for pigs, let alone people. But even so, we were all excited about having a real house of our own, and everybody worked very hard to clean it up and make it into a nice place to live. But it was only a little while, maybe a year, before we moved on again. I don't remember why we had to leave there, probably because we had to go where the work was."

Except for one brief period when another illegal immigrant lived with the family and took care of the children in exchange for room and board, the children accompanied their parents into the fields, where even the very young were expected to do their share. When they were little, they played more than they worked. "When my parents were picking tomatoes, I remember we'd sometimes go off where they couldn't see us and have tomato fights." As they grew, the balance shifted until, by adolescence, they were working alongside their parents and were expected to contribute a fair share to the daily earnings.

"I remember picking cherries when I was an adolescent," Ana recalls, her body stiffening as she describes the scene. As she speaks, I can see a young girl, her slim body encased in jeans, a sweat-soaked T-shirt clinging to her back, her face streaked with dirt as perspiration runs in rivulets down her cheeks. She makes her way carefully down a ladder, two big buckets filled with cherries hanging from a heavy leather strap around her neck. On the ground, she staggers slightly under their weight, then bends down low as she unhooks them, and, with a sigh of relief, dumps the cherries into a waiting box.

She stops a moment and looks around, wondering what time it is, how much longer this day will last. She has been picking cherries for hours and has made dozens of trips up and down the ladder, the buckets around her neck empty on the way up, full on the way down. Now, she's hot, tired, and thirsty. She wants to rest but knows she can't. Instead, she bends down, hooks the buckets to the strap, straightens up, and walks to the ladder. The cycle begins again.

"The work was so hard," says Ana when she finishes her story. "It took maybe four buckets to fill one of those boxes. I think they paid $1.75 for a box of cherries, which is a lot of working hours for very little money. I can still remember how tired I was afterward," she says, her shoulders sagging as if she can feel once again the weight of those buckets hanging from her neck. "It's a very hard way to make a living, and it can be dangerous, too. Once I lost my footing, and the ladder slipped out from under me. I grabbed a limb and hung on until my dad heard my screams and put the ladder back underneath me so I could get down."

She stops speaking for a few moments, seeming to be lost in her own thoughts. Then, shaking her head sorrowfully, she continues, "It's sad how people who work in agriculture are trapped there. That's all my family knew, and it's all we kids knew. You don't even think about options. Now when I think about it, it seems terrible that kids live like that. But then I was proud that I was good at picking those cherries and that my mom and dad recognized that I was a really good worker."

Even in California, agricultural work is seasonal, which meant that winter often brought even harder times than usual. During those periods, Yolanda Delgado was sometimes able to find work cleaning houses, while her husband picked up odd jobs. "But no matter what, my parents always managed to get enough money to feed us," recalls Ana, her words tinged with respect for their accomplishment. "It was very simple food, a lot of beans and rice, but we didn't go hungry."

It wasn't only transience, hard work, poverty, and outhouses that made Ana's life so difficult. There was no respite, no escape from suffering anywhere, since life inside the family was as harsh as it was outside. "My parents couldn't really give to anyone. I'm not sure if that has to do with their economic situation or if it's something that goes way back to when they were children and weren't given love either. All I know is they couldn't give us anything, not even a little comfort when we needed it."

Not only were her parents emotionally ungenerous, they were also rigidly authoritarian, demanding immediate and unquestioning obedience from their children. Any lapse was cause for severe punishment, especially by her father, whose explosive rages terrified the whole family. "I was always very frightened of my father," she recalls. "He was very much like the old stereotypic Latin—hot tempered, macho. We tried to avoid him, to stay away from him when he'd get like that. But you never knew what would set him off, so there was no way to protect yourself. You could be in dire need of comfort, and what you'd get would be violence.

"One time when we were living in that little house, there was a field right next to it where there were all kinds of wild cats. My dad warned me not to play with them. But I was just a little kid, no more than four or five, and I wanted one so badly. So one day I tried to pick one of the cats up, and it scratched me—a real deep wound in my thigh. I still have the scar on my leg. It was bleeding very hard, and I was terrified, so I ran home to tell my parents. But instead of comforting me, my dad lost it. He screamed at me: 'Didn't I tell you not to play with the cats?' I think I must have answered him back, which was something you weren't allowed to do. But I was just trying to explain what happened, and he got very, very angry and grabbed me by the hair and flung me around and around," she says, waving her arm in a wide circle above her head to demonstrate. Her words catch in her throat, and she pauses for a moment or two, then continues, "When he finally let go, I flew into the wall and got badly banged up."

She stops again, caught between anger and tears, then concludes sadly, "I think I was very depressed as a child, but I very rarely spoke up about my own feelings. What was the point? No one would understand if I did. Anyhow, I wasn't allowed to. My dad didn't allow independent thoughts."

For Ana, escape came by way of her dreams. While her parents and siblings remained rooted in the real world, she cultivated her internal one, a world in which life was limited by her imagination alone. "I always felt different, like nobody in my family understood me and like I didn't belong there, so I became very introspective. I used to think about running away, but I didn't know where to go. So I'd climb up a tree and sit there for hours, just sitting and thinking about how I wanted to be someplace else. Or sometimes I'd hide under my bed and spend a good part of the day there."

She dreamed about living in another family, one where she would feel understood, where she would have parents who would nurture and love her. She fantasized about living a different life in a new place, although she knew so little about the world outside her own that she had only the fuzziest image of what that life would look like.

In this world of her own creation, Ana could be free. Sometimes, when her father was raging, she imagined she was flying, hovering near the ceiling just out of his reach. Each time he lunged for her, she would fly a little higher, a little farther, triumphant in her ability to thwart him. A child's fantasy, to be sure, and also a vivid illustration of her refusal, even if in imagination alone, to be the passive victim of circumstance.

It's true, the wings she grew were illusory, but it's just such creative acts of imagination that were important in Ana's transcendence. In childhood, it was this ability that allowed her to picture another life when others around her could not—a creative feat that made a difference in how she fared in the life she actually had to live. Later, as an adult, it was the same imaginative capacity to envision possibilities that enabled her to seize the alternatives when they actually came into view.

While her daydreams brought relief from the stark realities of daily life, the nights were filled with terror, although even now she remains uncertain whether her fears were real or imagined. "I've always had the feeling that I was sexually molested by my father. I don't have any specific memories of actually being raped or anything. But I have this vague memory where he's hovering over me in my bed, and I'm hiding under my blankets, frightened and curled up in a ball, trying to make myself as small and insignificant as possible so he won't notice me. Then I hear my mom's voice calling out to him, 'Where are you? Come back to bed,' and he leaves.

"As a child it felt like my mom's voice calling him back saved me. When I think about it now, I wonder, *Where did she think he was, and what did she think he was doing?*" she asks, her words touched with bitterness.

Is the memory real, or is it a child's mind playing tricks? There was plenty of reason to fear her father in the daylight hours—his unpredictable temper, his cruelty, and his physical abuse. But why this nighttime scenario, vague, unformed, with nothing to back it up? These are questions Ana asked herself for years. Then recently, a dream, graphic in its presentation, put flesh on the skeleton of her childhood memory. "It was so real that I woke up scared as if I was that same little girl. I was a child in the dream, and the feeling was just like I remembered; it was like I was experiencing the whole thing over again. Only this time he came to my bed and woke me up. I was terrified, but I couldn't make a sound. He pulled off my underwear and grabbed me by the ankles while he was pulling down his pants. I guess he sensed my fear because he said, 'You won't feel a thing.' Then he held me by the arms and pulled me toward him and penetrated me. I couldn't say or do anything, but in my mind I kept hearing his words saying, 'You won't feel a thing; you won't feel a thing.' "

Real or imagined? To this day Ana wonders, sometimes convinced that her dream was a reenactment of a real experience, at other times doubtful. It's a question to which she may never find the answer. Although Carlos Delgado has been dead for several years, his ghost still haunts the family he dominated for so long. So when, shortly after she had the dream, Ana tried to talk to her mother and sisters, hoping they could provide a reality check about her memories, they refused to hear what she had to say.

Ana is hurt and angered by their response. But it shouldn't have surprised her, given the lifetime of failed relationships among her siblings. In a family where life is so arduous psychologically and physically, it's not unusual that siblings, too, become distant, preoccupied with their own fears and unmet needs, unable to give much to each other.

So it was in the Delgado family where, although there were four children, they provided little comfort for each other. "There was no one I could turn to. My siblings and I didn't know how to communicate with each other. How could we? There were no models around us of how to be good to each other, so we were modeling how my parents were to each other and to us. We were pretty much at each other's throat, each of us taking care of ourselves and not concerned about the other."

Since the human world was so uncharitable, Ana turned to the nonhuman one for the comfort and support she needed. There she found consolation in Woowy, a dog, who, she says, "was a lot more sensitive than the people around me." It was Woowy who sustained her through the pain, who was unfailingly there with his love, who became the companion of her heart. When her father hurt her, Woowy stood by and licked her tears. When she needed someone to confide in, Woowy listened. "I really loved that dog," Ana says. "When I was hurt, he'd just stay right by me. I'd look at him and see my sadness reflected in his eyes. I swear I even saw tears in his eyes when he saw me crying. He was the only one in the family who had any real connection to me or who seemed to understand me."

Friendships, too, were hard to sustain, partly because her father kept such tight control over the children's activities. "You couldn't keep friends because we were tied very much to the house. My dad didn't allow us to go to anyone else's house to play. So if I had friends, and I did have some, I would only be able to play with them at school. You can't really have friends that way."

But it wasn't her father's rules alone that made maintaining friendships a problem. It was also the prejudice against Mexican immigrants—prejudice that left Ana feeling ashamed of her parents' foreign ways. Indeed, this is one of the uncounted costs of the prejudice and discrimination immigrants meet when they come to this land of their dreams. In their wish to become real Americans, to be accepted by the world around them, the children adopt the public attitudes as their own and try to protect themselves from the barbs and the jeers by distancing themselves from their heritage and shrinking from any public expression of their difference.

I still remember how much I wanted to be an ordinary American, not Jewish, not the child of Russian immigrants who could barely speak English, just a plain vanilla American, someone whose name didn't set her apart, someone who ate peanut butter and jelly sandwiches instead of *gefilte fish*. I'm saddened now when I recall how I cringed when I heard my mother's accented English in public, how mortified I was when she came to school, how reluctant I was to ask my American friends into my home for fear that they'd sneer at what they saw and heard there.

Ana Guttierez, too, was embarrassed about her parents and uncomfortable about bringing Anglo friends home. "There were very few Mexicans in my school," she explains, "so I got a lot of teasing from the Anglo kids, even those who were my friends, because we were different. They thought something as simple as eating beans, our kind of food, was strange. So if they were ever around when my mother was cooking, they'd make some remark about the food. Or they'd hear my mother speaking Spanish and they'd say it sounds like babbling."

Ana also now looks back at these childhood feelings with chagrin, wishing that these things hadn't mattered so much then. But they matter for children in immigrant families, not only because of the shame the children feel but because when they hear their parents struggle with English, their child's faith in their parents' omnipotence, in their ability to care for and protect them, is shaken. If the adults in the family can't make their way comfortably in the world, can't make themselves easily understood, they are diminished in their children's eyes, unworthy of the trust that they can offer the protection every child needs.

The difficulties Ana encountered because of her Spanish-speaking Mexican heritage was only one part of the problem. Being agricultural workers brought yet another level of torment. "The kids from farm families were really stigmatized. It was terrible what we went through. There was never a time at school when there wasn't some racial slur hurled at me," recalls Ana. "We were called all kinds of names: taco, burrito, beaners, wetbacks. And many times we were chased after school and stoned, actually stoned. Some of the Mexican kids survived by fighting. Thank God I was slender and had long legs. I escaped by outrunning them."

In this atmosphere, Spanish, the language that greeted her at birth, that framed her world in infancy and early childhood, was abandoned in favor of English, the language of the other, *los gringos*. "You can't help it; you begin to feel very ashamed of your language and your culture," explains Ana, her voice tight, her eyes clouded with the pain of remembering the taunts and humiliations of those years. "It was such a negative thing that I wanted to forget I was Mexican. So more and more, as I experienced so much prejudice and discrimination, I refused to speak Spanish, even at home."

But giving up a language is no small psychological feat. When we learn a language, we absorb more than its words and its syntax. Embedded in each language is a way of thinking about the world, of meeting it, of being in it. To give it up, therefore, means relinquishing a part of yourself, the part that experienced the world through that language.

For Ana, the task was made somewhat easier by her early rejection of her family. "I knew I didn't want to be like them, and I didn't want to do things like they did." If *they* embodied the language and culture of Mexico, *she* would be something else. By eschewing the language, therefore, she could accomplish two goals: She could distance herself still further from the family, thereby reinforcing her sense of being different and, with it, keeping alive her dreams of escape. At the same time, she could hope to still her tormentors by becoming more like them.

The first part worked; she became progressively more isolated and marginal in the family. But, as she would learn all too quickly, no matter what language she spoke, she was still identifiably Mexican, still the child of migrant farmworkers, still the alien other upon whom *real* Americans could vent their prejudice and frustrations.

It wasn't until her late teens, when the resurgence of ethnic pride among America's minorities helped young people like Ana to reclaim their heritage, that she was ready to own being Mexican again. "Then I wanted to get more in touch with my culture and I became proud of it. I wanted to find out more about it and also relearn the language, which I had nearly forgotten by then."

Isolated, lonely, frightened, outsider—these are the words and the feelings that define Ana's childhood and adolescence. She dreamed of getting out, of finding another life. But what would it be? When her older sister got a scholarship to college, her father forbid her to accept it. His daughters, he insisted, would marry, bear children, and serve their husbands quietly and faithfully. "They had these terrible fights," says Ana, her voice choked with emotion as she recalls the scene. "He'd hit her, and she'd try to hit back, but he'd get the best of her and really beat her up." She pauses, trying to regain control; then, closing her eyes as if to blot out the memory, she says, "It was terrible, just terrible; I don't think I can tell you how terrible it was."

Frightened by the violence, believing that there was no other exit, Ana took the only path she could. "I had just turned eighteen. I'd watched what my sister went through and I didn't want to go that route; it was too scary. I didn't see any other way out of the house, so I got married."

Like her, Ana's new husband, Ramon Guttierez, came from a family of farmworkers; like her, he had worked in the fields all his life. For Ana, therefore, the contours of daily life changed little. She continued to pick fruits and vegetables, only now she worked next to her husband instead of her father. The big change came when she became pregnant with her daughter, Angela. As a family, they became eligible for one of the units of subsidized housing the government had recently built, a move that would take them out of the migrant-labor camps and into a home of their own. "Since it was subsidized housing, you didn't need any down payment, and the rent was real cheap. It was a brand-new house; it was little, but it was adequate. The neighborhood, though, that was terrible. Not many people wanted to live out there, so they built this subsidized housing for low-income people.

"It was like a ghetto. Well, I never lived in a ghetto, but it seemed like that. There were thugs and drug dealers all over the neighborhood. We'd get our house vandalized a couple of times a month, so we had to put bars on the windows. I hated that; it made me feel caged up."

Since the house was in the city, they were dependent on contractors who were hired by farmers to supply workers when they were needed. The contractors, who knew Ramon as a good worker, would let him know when help was needed, and he'd gather together Ana and some of his brothers, pile them into his car, and drive out to the field.

Life went along uneventfully for several years, the young couple living the only life they knew. Ramon replaced Ana's father as the voice of authority in the household. She, as befitted a traditional Mexican wife, worked in the fields all day and cooked, cleaned, and tended her husband and child at night. "I was a young adult, about twenty-three, and I still didn't know any better," Ana says, her eyes wide in disbelief as she recalls the woman she once was. "I guess I just did what I had to do, what my culture expected me to do.

"But then something happened. We were picking onions. Did you ever see how onions grow? The onion is the root; it has a real firm hold on the earth. They're very low growing, so you have to stoop down and yank them out and throw them into this big burlap bag you're dragging along behind you. After a while, your back hurts terribly, so you get on your knees. Then your knees give out, and by the end of the day, you're on all fours. It's horrible, backbreaking work. I'd have all kinds of rashes on my arms and face and neck—every place that was exposed. That was the point when I began to think, *'I have to do something better.'*"

Obviously, it wasn't just the agony of picking onions that day that enabled Ana to see the possibility of another life. She had, after all, picked onions often before without such an epiphany. But by then, the impact of the feminist revolution had filtered down even to the Imperial Valley of California. It's not that Ana had any conscious thoughts about feminism or its influence on her life. But the transformation of the society in response to the feminist agitation of the previous decade opened up vistas she couldn't have dreamed of earlier.

Television, women's magazines, and the press were all trumpeting the changes in women's lives, news she grasped at hungrily, her imagination fired by the possibilities. "Until then I didn't have any role models, not even in school. But then the media began providing models for women that were different. I'd watch TV or read a magazine and I'd see women doing all kinds of things. That was real significant in giving me permission to think about doing some of those things.

"I guess what was going on until then was that I had two cultures inside of me, and they were at odds with each other. One was the very traditional Mexican culture, which, for a long time, was very dominant. But part of me was also American. That was mostly suppressed by the Mexican side until I began to see American women all over the media doing interesting things. By then, I guess I had also begun to see the faults and flaws in the marriage and the Mexican culture, so the American side began to come out of hiding. It was like seeing those women going to school and working and pursuing their own lives opened my eyes."

Not surprisingly, Ramon much preferred Ana's eyes to stay closed. As long as she was naive and docile, accepting her traditional role, bowing to his authority, things were fine. But when Ana decided she wanted to make her own decisions about what she would do with her life, the trouble began. "When I started becoming more my own person and wanting to pursue my own interests, which were more modern and more American, that was very threatening to him."

By "more modern and more American," Ana means that she wanted to find another kind of work, perhaps go back to school—an idea that was unthinkable to Ramon. It wasn't that he objected to his wife working outside the home. She had, after all, been doing so for years. But working in the fields kept her in his sphere of influence and under his watchful eye. "Those men want a woman where they can watch her all the time because they're jealous and afraid she'll stray," Ana explains. "And also," she adds snidely, "so that she's around to meet all their needs all the time."

Once she had made her decision, however, Ana would not be deterred. Months of conflict followed until she and Ramon finally reached a compromise. If she worked only part time and didn't neglect him or the household, he agreed to allow her to try to find work in a school. "A job in a school was okay because there were only women and children," she says irritably.

Ana quickly found a job as a teacher's aide in a bilingual classroom. There she soon proved to be a talented and imaginative teacher, not only teaching English to the children but developing a variety of activities to promote their cultural awareness while easing them into life as Americans. She smiles with pleasure when she speaks of this period—pleasure because she had finally escaped the drudgery of picking fruit, because she was doing work that tapped capacities she hadn't known existed, because she was helping children like herself to enter a new world with less grief than she had suffered. "With the Spanish-speaking kids, I could really be helpful in easing them into the English-only environment. I couldn't do that so well with the kids who weren't Spanish speaking, like the kids who spoke Farsi, because I didn't speak their language or understand their culture," she adds with a note of sadness.

"It was really wonderful. I was actually helping to change the things that were such a torment for me when I started school as a non-English-speaking child. I think I might have had a different feeling about my culture and my language if there had been some kind of bilingual program like that then. So in a roundabout way, I was helping to heal myself."

The job not only boosted Ana's self-confidence, the teachers and administrators she met there provided her with the first live models of independent professional women who were committed to their work, as well as to their families. It wasn't long before she began to think about becoming professional herself. "I worked with these teachers and got to know them and saw what was possible," she says. "So after a while I became dissatisfied with the job because I was doing just as much work as the teachers, and I saw myself just as competent as them, but I wasn't getting paid nearly as much. That's when I decided I was going to go to college. And that's when my marriage really began to go downhill and unravel."

For Ana, going to school meant that she worked on the job all day; came home to what sociologist Arlie Hochschild has called "the second shift" of household and child care tasks; then when everything was done, left to go to class, this time to a chorus of complaints from her husband. Although she started by taking only one evening class at a local junior college, Ramon made it as difficult as possible for her. He refused to take care of their daughter, forcing Ana to take the child with her or to find some relative to baby-sit. If she rushed the after-dinner cleanup so as not to be late for class, he'd complain that the dishes weren't washed properly. If he saw her studying, he'd insist that she was neglecting her household duties.

At first, the schoolwork itself was very hard for Ana. The public schools she had attended earlier failed to provide her with an adequate foundation in such essential subjects as English and mathematics. Her first year, therefore, was spent in remedial classes trying to catch up. But nothing—not her educational handicaps, not the difficulty of being a student while working and caring for her family, not her husband's angry demands, not even her realization that she was courting disaster in her marriage if she continued on her chosen path—could dim her determination and her excitement about the adventure she had embarked upon.

Her academic deficits notwithstanding, Ana quickly proved herself an outstanding student, winning encouragement and recognition from her teachers and earning scholarships that eased her financial way. With each success, Ramon's anger escalated. "He started to drink, and he'd come home at three in the morning, making all kinds of noise—blasting the music, things like that—and start to push me around. With all the noise, my daughter would wake up and come out scared, but he'd pick her up and throw her into her room. It was terrible. She'd be screaming in her room and listening to him shout all kinds of abusive things at me while he was throwing things around, breaking up the place. Most of the time he'd rape me, too, force himself on me in that disgusting drunken state." She stops speaking, her face a mask of revulsion, then says with quiet, firm conviction, "The best thing I've ever done for myself was to leave him."

But leaving wasn't easy. She kept threatening; he kept begging her forgiveness and promising to change. She relented; life returned to normal for a week or two. Inevitably, he'd start to drink again, and the nightmare would resume.

It took two more long years of abuse before she was finally able to move from threat to reality. During that time, he browbeat and humiliated her repeatedly. He tormented her with threats to show up in class and haul her out bodily if necessary. "It made me nervous, but I figured it was just a threat. Then one night he actually did show up. He came into the classroom and stood there looking very angry. He didn't have to say anything; I just left. But I was so embarrassed, so shamed."

Sometimes when he decided he didn't want her to go out, he imprisoned her in the house. "The house was like a prison cell, with bars on the windows and the kind of locks where you needed a key to get out. He took my keys and locked me in there with Angela. We were totally trapped in there, no way to get out. If there had been a fire, we'd have been burned alive."

Even after she took her daughter and left, the harassment didn't stop. He stalked her, threatened her, and attempted to kidnap her. Nothing stopped him, not the restraining order she got, not her threats to put him behind bars. Finally, after a wild ride when he tried to run her off the road, she filed a complaint, whereupon he was charged with assault with a deadly weapon and spent several months in jail.

Although he continued to try to hound her after his release, a reminder that she could send him back to jail was enough to make him keep some distance. "He never did anything like that again," says Ana, "but for about a year or so after that, he tried to manipulate me through Angela by telling her how much he missed being with us and how it was all my fault. It was hard when she'd come home and say, 'Daddy's really sad and wants you back. Why won't you take him back, mom?' But by then I knew what I had to do."

Within a year of her separation, Ana qualified for early entrance to the undergraduate program at one of the University of California campuses. "I was really grateful to be able to get away from everything and move here with Angela, just the two of us." Just the two of them, however, had its own problems. From the time she became pregnant, Ana knew the kind of parent she wanted to be. "I had a plan in place; I was going to be a really caring, loving, nurturing parent, different than they were to me," she says.

But for people who have been inadequately nurtured in their own early childhood, there's often a gap between their wishes and what they're able to do for their own children. So there were times, particularly when Angela was sick and needy, when Ana simply couldn't be there as fully as her child needed. "I couldn't help it; I didn't have it to give, and I disengaged. How I wish there was a way to do it over again."

What parent doesn't know the wish "to do it over again," to have a second chance, to correct the mistakes of the past. For me, it was particularly poignant to listen to Ana's regrets, for they so closely mirrored my own. I, too, had promised myself that I would give my daughter all the loving kindness I had been denied. I, too, found myself unable to fulfill the promise as well as I would have liked, especially in my child's infancy.

I wish I could blame the postpartum illness that incapacitated me for the first few months of her life. But although that undoubtedly played a part, the deeper problem lay in the profound psychological injury I suffered in my own childhood. My child's utter dependence, the depth of her need, touched my own unmet needs and found there a well of yearning and resentment I hadn't known existed. I remember looking down at her as she slept in her crib, my heart torn between love, fear, and resentment. *How can you ask so much when I've had so little?* I wanted to cry. *Please don't let me hurt her as I've been hurt,* I begged a God I didn't believe in.

It wasn't that I was a bad mother, any more than Ana was. Like her, I steeled myself to do what had to be done. And most of the time I pulled it off with no one but me the wiser. But like Ana, I'll never fully forgive myself for being unable, in those first months of my daughter's life, to mother her with the generosity of spirit she deserved.

For Ana, the difficulty in parenting was complicated by a conflict between her intuitive sense of her child's needs and the demands of a traditional culture. "Until I left my husband, she was raised in the traditional Mexican way, at least the only way my husband and I knew. You tell children what to do and expect to be obeyed, and when you're not, they get a spanking. It's something I'd never do now; it's not part of me anymore. I was never real comfortable with it, but it was all I knew."

After the separation, Ana decided to take some parenting classes, partly because she wanted to learn about "how Americans raise children," and partly because she was afraid that, with all the stress, her difficulty in being an emotionally present parent would escalate. "Even though Ramon never took care of her, it was different, harder, being a single parent. And I was afraid I couldn't really be a good and present parent. Also I wanted to learn about more modern parenting practices. I didn't know anything about that, like giving children choices instead of telling them what to do and expecting them to do it. That's not at all a part of my culture."

By the time she left the Imperial Valley for university life, Ana was well on the way to becoming the parent she wanted to be. She was twenty-seven and Angela was seven when they set off on what seemed to both of them a great adventure. For the first time in Ana's life, she was free—free to raise her child as she wished, to live where she wanted, to go where she chose, to see whom she pleased. She made friends, dated men, and began to develop a new and enlarged sense of herself. But nothing interfered with her progress at school, where she continued to do exceptionally well, earning scholarships and grants that, together with her stipend from Aid to Families with Dependent Children (AFDC), provided the financial support she needed to pursue her goals.

During this period, Ana, who had left the Catholic church in which she was raised, began to feel a need for a spiritual life. Her quest led her to the New Age movement, where she found a program that promoted self-healing by way of meditation, affirmations, channeling energy, and the laying on of hands. "After I left my husband, I started to do a lot of work on my past and on my emotional life. What really helped was taking a program, maybe two years or so, in the healing arts. The techniques I was taught there are very spiritual, as well as psychological.

"I used to be very angry, especially at my father. But a lot of the work I did helped me to change that anger to acceptance, and I'm more at peace with my past now. I also had to learn to love myself; I'm still learning, in fact, and still use some of those natural healing techniques, although I'm not involved in any program or anything like that anymore."

Three years after she entered the university, she earned her bachelor's degree in psychology and went immediately into a master's program. By then, she was living with Russell, who had abandoned a career as a successful executive recruiter to pursue a doctorate. "He's had a riches-to-rags kind of life," Ana says with a smile. "But he has no regrets; he's doing what he wants to do. It's amazing, isn't it, what people are willing to give up to pursue their dreams!" she exclaims in wide-eyed wonder.

Unlike Ana's earlier relationships with men, she and Russell were friends before they became lovers. "Before Russell, I didn't have any friendships with men, only with women. But Russell was my friend for a long time before we got together sexually. So we have lots in common and can have this really good, supportive relationship. It's really wonderful. We both love children and are very into family. I didn't know people could be so loving," she sighs with satisfaction.

It's now about a year since I first met Ana. Her relationship with Russell remains an enormous source of gratification, and their three children—hers, his, and theirs—are thriving in an atmosphere of love and concern that Ana could only dream about in her own childhood. With the end of Russell's schooling on the horizon, wedding plans are in the air. "We couldn't get married until he finished and got a job because I would have lost my AFDC and we needed that to live," Ana explains. "But now he'll be able to support us, and I won't be dependent on government assistance anymore."

Academically, she has been a star. She graduated from her master's program with her department's highest award and won a highly prized fellowship in a first-rate doctoral program. "I'd like to combine psychology with spirituality, but right now I'm not sure how I can do it or exactly what my focus will be," she says. Like so many of the others in this book, however, a sense of mission guides her plan for the future. So while she isn't certain exactly what shape her professional life will take, she does know that she'll be working with children and families, doing work that, she hopes, will spare others the pain she has suffered.

The conflict of cultures Ana describes as part of her earlier years has abated as she has more fully integrated her Mexican and American sides. In her way of being a woman in the world, in her aspirations for herself and her daughters, in the kind of egalitarian family life she and Russell have organized, she's distinctly American. But in a part of her soul that America can't reach, she's also a Mexican Indian. It's visible in the kind of inner calm that's so much a part of her, in the patience that a thousand years of Indian culture breeds, in her fascination with the spiritual elements of Native American culture, in the soapstone sculptures she carves, in the mandalas she crafts, in the beaded elk-hide dress she has been working on for two years, in the native themes she paints on leather. "I'm not just Mexican, I'm Indian," she says with as much pride as she takes in her accomplishments of the past decade. "My mother has forgotten that part of our ancestry, but it's a very deep part of me. That's why my connection to Native American art and culture seems very natural; it's recapturing that part of my own cultural identity."

Ana remains the outsider in her family, the only one who has left her past so far behind. Her brother, the only boy in the family, died at eighteen in an automobile accident under suspicious circumstances. Was he under the influence of alcohol? Drugs? No one is sure. Her sisters live in relatively traditional marriages and work at low-level jobs. Her relationships with them, as well as with her mother, are strained and distant as Ana continues to feel unheard and misunderstood, just as she did as a child.

Like the other women and men in this book, Ana has moments when she can still feel the pain and loneliness that comes with being the marginal one. Like them, too, she understands that it's this very quality that made her early life so difficult that also laid the groundwork for her later escape.

The psychological work Ana has done over the years has helped her make peace with her past—a peace held together sometimes by real acceptance, sometimes by denial, which serves as a cloak to protect her from the old pain. It's a fragile peace, capable of being broken when her family hurts or disappoints her, as they still do on those occasions when hope overtakes judgment and she turns to them for comfort or support. Then the denial slips, and the childhood pain and anger reemerge. But most of the time, her denial works well in helping her to sustain the life she has built by not allowing her past trauma to define her present reality.

Along with the denial, however, there's another quality that helps to account for Ana's resilience—one that shares company with denial but is also different from it. It's the capacity to limit the pain she allows herself to experience, to dole it out in doses small enough to be manageable emotionally. In fact, this is one of the qualities shared by people who transcend their past, the ability to control the amount of pain they feel, to put a lid on it when it threatens to overwhelm them.

This isn't a conscious act. Rather, it happens out of awareness, a protective defense that permits a person to withstand life's assaults without being flooded and disabled by the pain. By allowing it to come up in small doses, such people defer its full impact until they're in a situation where it's safe to feel it. By then, too, they're distant enough from the event so that the emotional response, no matter how intense, is both more muted and more time limited than it would have been earlier.

In my own life, this capacity to dole out the pain got me through a divorce with relatively little anguish. I don't mean that I felt no distress, only that I didn't suffer it intensely. At the time, I congratulated myself, convinced that I had been successful in working through the issues about the separation before leaving the marriage. Then, three years later, after I was remarried, an old friend who was in the midst of an agonizing divorce came to stay with us. I spent several days listening to her story, trying to ease her torment, all the while aware that something I couldn't grab hold of was nibbling at the edge of my consciousness. A few hours after she left, I was catapulted, without warning, into the feelings I had not allowed myself to experience during my own divorce. My friend's suffering had opened the floodgates of my denied pain—the fear, the anguish, the grief I couldn't allow myself to feel fully until the event was sufficiently distant and I was safe in a life that had already helped to heal many of the hurts of the past.

Given how far Ana has come in a single decade of her life—from twenty-three to thirty-three—it's not surprising that, when she reflects on how she got from there to here, it seems very sudden. "It feels as if it happened in one big jump, like I was just opening up, blossoming, from the time I left my marriage." But like the bud that becomes a flower or the caterpillar that turns into a butterfly, the foundation for such transformations is laid long before the event that seems so magical.

When we look at Ana's life, therefore, we can see that the path to her present was laid out in the past—in her early childhood when she understood and accepted her marginality in the family; when she hid in a tree so she could dream of another life without interruption; when she constructed a meaningful relationship with her dog when there was none to be found with the people around her; when she refused to be totally cowed by her father, just as she would later stand her ground before her husband.

Her formidable psychological strengths notwithstanding, her journey along that path was facilitated by the political and cultural movements of her time. It was the movement calling for ethnic pride that taught Ana to value her heritage, to savor it, to bring it into her life, and with it, to gain an enlarged and renewed sense of herself. Just so, it was the feminist movement that laid before her the possibility of alternatives she couldn't have imagined earlier. True, it was her capacity to dream, to imagine herself in those new roles, that allowed her to move into them. But without such movements to widen the imaginative possibilities, her choices would have been substantially restricted.

seven

Kevin McLaren: Musical Genius

I FEEL THE STING OF TEARS AS KEVIN MCLAREN PLAYS THE CLOSING notes of the Prelude from Bach's C Minor Cello Suite. "That was beautiful," I say, to the small, almost delicate, thirty-six-year-old man who stands before me, his viola dangling at his side. He smiles with pleasure. "The words are great," he replies, "but I got what I wanted when I saw your tears."

I return his smile automatically while my mind is busy with questions: *How did this man, who grew up in a world of alcoholism, psychosis, and violence, get far enough away from the family pathology to be able to create such beauty? What role did his obvious talent play in his escape? How did he become a violist when he never saw a viola, or even knew classical music existed, until he discovered the music section in the public library when he was thirteen years old?*

"How did I know I was musical?" he asks, repeating the question I ask when I collect my wits. "I wish it were more complicated, but it's not. Some people can quote Shakespeare, which always impresses me. I have the same ability, but I do it in a different language.

"Music is a language in your head, just like the language you speak. And I guess I've felt a need to communicate in that language since I was a very little kid. It's always been there, swarming around in my head just like thoughts. If you're fortunate enough to put your hands on a musical instrument, as I was, you realize that you're playing those thoughts out, only you're speaking in another language."

For Kevin, as with any musically gifted person, the problem was giving form to the language, learning to make "words" out of the "thoughts" that kept running through his head—a problem magnified by his parents' total ignorance about music. "I come from a family that's cultureless," says Kevin. "No one in my family understands the first thing about music. It's just not a part of their world. Once they understood that I was serious about the piano, which is the instrument I started with, the best they could think of for me was that I'd grow up and play on the Lawrence Welk show. Even now," he concludes laughing, "my father still calls a classical piece a song."

From the outside, the McLaren family looked perfectly normal. Dennis McLaren, Kevin's father, was a small-businessman who devoted his life to providing a modest but stable financial base for his family. Katherine, his wife, was a housewife, who worked occasionally at small part-time jobs. They were two devoted parents who lived in a nice house in a good neighborhood with their two intelligent, healthy children. When the curtains parted, however, the view from the inside featured an alcoholic father, a mother suffering from manic depressive psychosis, and a household that could erupt in violence without warning. "My parents are a very dysfunctional couple," says Kevin matter-of-factly. "When I was a little kid I used to worry that they'd get divorced; as I grew older, I wanted them to divorce.

"My father would drink more than a six-pack of beer in an evening. He'd spend every night watching television and drinking beer. As a child, I never saw anything else, so it seemed like the normal thing to do. Now I know he had a problem with alcohol, and it has gotten worse through the years.

"I never saw him strike my mother, but sometimes when they were fighting, he'd become verbally abusive. It was a strange and confusing relationship. When I was a little kid, I remember times when they were very affectionate with each other. But there was also the other side, when they would fight terribly and say very hateful things to each other. That escalated through the years. There were times when my father would get so mad, he'd break down the door.

"It wasn't good practice for learning about relationships," he says with a rueful smile. "As a kid you wonder, is a relationship between two people like a pendulum—sometimes you love and sometimes you hate? Mostly when I was small, I didn't understand, and it seemed frightening because you never knew what to expect. When I got older, it just began to seem stupid, and I'd leave the house, go off on my own, and get away. I didn't want to hear it."

It wasn't only his father's alcoholism and his parents' conflictful and sometimes violent relationship from which Kevin sought escape, but his mother's mental illness as well. "My mother is manic depressive. There's lots of mental illness in her family," says Kevin, his voice reflective, as if once again he's trying to understand her illness. "Her father probably was manic depressive, and I have a feeling that several of my mother's aunts and uncles were, too. And my mother's older brother, there's some story of dysfunction there. In my whole life, I've never heard my uncle speak, but it's *never* talked about," he says, his tone registering his amazement.

Although Kevin's words tell of frightening events, his emotional tone as he relays them is as cool as if he were reporting what the family ate for breakfast. When I comment on his calm, unemotional recitation, he replies, "I've always felt like I was in some sort of bubble that kept me apart from my family. Yes, all that was going on around me, but there was a space inside where it didn't interfere or touch me; I just couldn't let it.

"So when they'd fight or my father would break down the door, I'd look at those things and all I could think was, *I don't ever want to be like that. I don't want to have a life like that.* I guess that's as close as I came to having a personal reaction where I identified with them." He pauses as he hears his words, then continues with a small smile, "Or, I guess you'd say, where I *didn't* identify with them.

"From the time I was very little, I felt like I had nothing in common with them, like I was a stranger who got there by accident. It was like being a dog who was growing up in the middle of a cat family. They never understood what I was about," he says mournfully. "They wanted me to go out and play with the other kids; all I wanted was to play the piano, and before that, I'd draw or paint or read books.

"It's the same with all my relatives," Kevin continues. "They're sweet, but I always felt like an alien when I was with them. I could never look at them and feel, *'That's my heritage.'* Even as a kid, when I'd go to a Christmas party with the family, it felt bizarre and I'd think, *How do I come to be at this gathering with these people?"*

He stops speaking and seems to be trying on his next thought. Finally, after several moments, he says reluctantly, "I don't want this to sound arrogant, but it's part of what made me who I am, so I have to say it." He hesitates again, as if waiting for a signal from me, then continues, "I think I knew very early that I was smarter than my parents, and they knew it, too. When I was very young, my father would try to help with my homework. But pretty soon he realized that I was farther along than he was, and he stopped altogether.

"The same thing happened with the piano. When I was about three years old, my aunt gave me a toy piano for Christmas. I spent all my time after that playing with it and asking for a real one. Finally, my parents bought a piano when I was about five. My mother could play a little bit, so she'd play and I'd watch. Pretty soon I could figure out what she was doing. Then I started to take lessons from this woman who used to play the organ at the roller-skating rink in town, and it wasn't long before I could play better than my mother could. The day she realized that, she never played again."

As I listen to his words, I wonder, *What is it like to have a child who surpasses you by the time he's seven years old?* But before my thoughts can take me any further, Kevin answers my unspoken question. "I think they were intimidated by me when I was a child; they still are. They never know what to say when I see them. As I got older and gained competence in more things, my parents backed out more and more. It was like they were afraid they wouldn't know what to say, so they never said anything but the simplest things—'Hi, how was your day? What did you do in school?' But they never talked about real things or about the things that interested me. I doubt that they had any idea what they were."

We can't know what Kevin's parents knew, of course. Yet it seems likely that they *did* know at least some of what interested him—music, for example, the piano, books, art. But their own knowledge of these things was so limited, there was little ground for conversation with a child who already knew so much more than they did. In fact, this is one of those families in which parents and child were profoundly mismatched—a misfit that left Kevin alienated and the McLarens struggling to understand a son who often seemed like a stranger to them.

Despite this unhappy circumstance, Kevin was a cherished child, one who, when he was still an infant, was struck with a near-fatal illness that intensified his parents' connection to him while it also helped to widen the gulf between them. As the child who miraculously survived, he became both a special kind of treasure and a constant source of worry. "My parents were so grateful that I didn't die that I was treated differently than my sister. It was like I was a very fragile commodity, the way some people treat the most valuable piece of porcelain. They don't want to touch it; they can stand back and admire it, but they're also afraid of it.

"In some ways, I suppose it was good to feel so loved and cared for," says Kevin hesitantly, his words touched with doubt. "In other ways it was a real problem," he concludes more resolutely. For this wasn't just love he felt. It was the kind of hovering concern that so often marks the treatment of a child who has survived a life-threatening illness, a part of the family ethos that generates its own set of problems.

For Kevin, the kind of look-but-don't-touch uneasiness he describes created around him a special aura that heightened his sense of being different and helped to separate him still further from the rest of the family. For his sister, Susan, who was born into a family in which her brother's illness made him the focus of everyone's anxious attention, it stimulated an intense rivalry she could never win, a rivalry the parents tried to mediate by splitting the children between them. "My sister became my father's child, and I was my mother's," says Kevin, a resolution that only deepened the conflict between the children and isolated them further from one another.

Whatever the other issues and conflicts in the family, however, they paled before Katherine McLaren's mental illness, which dominated the daily life of the household as far back as her son can remember. When he was little, the family lore was that her problems were connected to her menstrual period, during which she suffered migraine headaches and severe cramps. Each month, therefore, she took to her bed for several days. But when, in her early thirties, she had a hysterectomy, her problems didn't end.

By the time Kevin was eleven years old, his mother began what he characterizes as "her serious slide downward." More and more she needed drugs to stay calm, Valium at first, then more powerful tranquilizers; finally, when her manic depression was diagnosed, lithium. But nothing was fully effective in maintaining her stability, as she swung without warning from the depressive to the manic side.

"She'd have periods when nothing could make her happy, and their arguments became bigger and bigger. They'd have an argument, and she'd spend three days in bed with the blinds drawn. Then she'd get up; they'd make up; things were okay for a few weeks; then it would start again. All that increased my father's alcohol consumption and made them more and more dysfunctional as a couple," Kevin recalls, the tension in his voice giving the lie to his surface composure.

When she was on the manic side, she was, in her son's words, "happy, silly, wild. She would be superactive; everything was larger than life," he says, throwing his arms wide in a gesture that seeks to encompass the world. "She'd get involved in all kinds of things and projects, but she could never follow through with anything because she'd hit a depressive cycle. So she might join a women's club and for a couple of months be on a manic high, then she'd hit the depression and she'd never go back again."

When his mother fell into one of her depressions, "it was quiet time in the house." Everything stopped; everyone else's needs were put on hold; normal childhood activity was forbidden as the children were enjoined from doing anything that might disturb their mother. "My sister and I would have to be very quiet and stay in our respective rooms and color or read or things like that.

"I remember being in my room and hearing her moaning my name, calling me to come. I'd go in, and from under all these covers she'd stick a hand out with an ice pack and ask me to fill it. I'd go to the kitchen, fill it, and bring it back, and she'd put it on her head. Or she'd ask me to make her a piece of toast, which I'd do." He pauses a moment; then, anticipating the question I'm about to ask, he says in a tone uncharacteristically sharp, "How did I feel about being her caretaker? It just seemed like part of life."

He stops talking again, looks around the room as if trying to distract himself, and continues, "In later years, she'd become quite violent. Once she attacked my father with a knife and tried to kill him. The police came and took my mother away in an ambulance. My father needed stitches to close his wounds that time, and my mother was in a psych ward for two weeks," he concludes, closing his eyes as if to erase the memory.

It's not uncommon in families like Kevin's for children to feel guilty, as if they are somehow at fault for a mother's illness, a father's alcoholism, their parents' conflicts. But Kevin had no such illusions. The separation he established early in his life, the boundaries between himself and his parents he tended so carefully, held firm no matter what the provocation. It was as if he was separated by a glass barrier—a bubble, he calls it—that only he knew existed, a barrier that allowed him to be present physically but absent psychologically, to see and hear but not fully feel what was happening on the other side. "I was no more than five or six when I could look at my parents and say, 'That's them; this is me.' I was always able to see that separation very distinctly. I had to; it was necessary to preserve myself from an environment that would have destroyed me if I couldn't do that."

But saying that he "had to" maintain the separation tells us only what was, not how he managed it. To do it, he had to remove himself psychologically, to *dis*identify, to become an observer of the family rather than a participant in it. In this endeavor, a well-developed sense of humor helped. "I could always see both the humor and the pathos in the melodrama that was such a part of my family. That was my defense, I suppose, one of my ways of preserving myself," he says.

It's a useful defense. The ability to laugh at the incongruity of the family drama enabled him to maintain enough distance to keep from being sucked in and overwhelmed by it. But laughter alone is not enough. As he stood aside and watched, Kevin understood that he had no control over the chaos and insanity that framed family life in the McLaren household. This is a frightening acknowledgment for a child, one most children avoid knowing. Instead, they keep trying to control the uncontrollable, to fix the unfixable, each failure sinking them deeper into the muck of the family pathology as their definition of the problem shifts from "It's them. Why don't they stop doing what they do?" to "It's me. Why can't I make it better?"

But somehow Kevin knew that road led nowhere. So he bent his efforts to developing the capacity to stand back and distinguish what was his problem, what was theirs; what he could fix, what he couldn't. "I realized very early that one of the most important things in life is for me to be able to identify what are my responsibilities, what belongs to someone else. If someone's angry, does it belong to them or to me? If I did something that caused someone to feel angry with me, I can take responsibility for that. But if they're angry about something else and are trying to set that in my lap, I don't have to take it if I know which part is mine and which is theirs. If it's mine, I can fix it; if it belongs to someone else, it's out of my control."

Although this ability to maintain clear boundaries between self and other enabled Kevin to survive, the cost of the separation was a deep and pervasive loneliness that wasn't eased until he was old enough to find others in the world outside with whom he could connect—a teacher, an older friend, another family, each of them helping to point the direction to a different life. "I wanted out of that world so much, but it wasn't until I got older that I began to find people I could relate to and who helped me get out."

Indeed, Kevin's ability to seek help and to recognize people who could give it has been a central element in his transcendence. But he wouldn't have met with such success if those others hadn't been willing partners in the enterprise. It's precisely because he has the quality of adoptability that I've spoken of throughout these narratives— because he's so likable, as well as so smart and talented—that he has been able to draw people to him who were happy to become his teachers and mentors.

In elementary school, it was the music teacher who reached out to him with special favor and attention. When the other children were playing in the schoolyard after lunch, she let him come into the classroom to play the piano. In junior high school, it was the director of the school orchestra who recognized and encouraged his special talent.

"Each time one of those people crossed my path," says Kevin, "I'd follow the current to the next one. And music surely was the thing that changed my life. It gave me the ticket out of my family and that whole environment. I've been all over the world; I've been able to live a totally different life from the one I grew up in. None of that would have been possible without music."

For a man who would become a classical musician, his early musical education was unorthodox, to say the least. He quickly surpassed his first teacher, who taught him all she knew about the kind of popular tunes that provided the background music in the roller-skating rink where she performed. "I got through all the books very fast and started to get frustrated. I was playing this popular music, which was okay, but I didn't *feel* anything about it. I kept thinking, *There has to be something more.* But I didn't know about classical music."

Finally, when he was thirteen, he discovered the music section of the public library. Wide eyed, he wandered around the stacks, pulling out one volume after another, running his fingers over the notes on the page, listening to the music they made in his head. "It was my first discovery of classical music. I was in awe standing in this huge room surrounded by music," he says, his expression reflecting the wonder he felt then. "I was so excited I could hardly breathe. I asked the librarian where the piano music was, and she showed me this whole wall of it. I couldn't believe my eyes."

That was the beginning of Kevin's classical music training. He checked out some music and began to teach himself to play it. Soon he was playing piano in the orchestra of his junior high school. Not long after, the director, impressed by both his determination and his talent, arranged for his first public concert—an event that connected him to a young cellist, Laura Lowenthal, and her family, who would become central figures in Kevin's musical development.

"The director knew Laura, who was still in elementary school, and she wanted me to do a concert with her. She gave me the music, and after I learned my part, Laura's parents brought her to my house so we could practice. The minute they walked in the door, I knew something special had happened. My parents knew it, too. I remember them standing in the doorway of the room where we were practicing and looking scared and like they were totally out of place, even though it was happening in their house. But all I could think of when I looked at that family was, *This is where I belong.* "

The Lowenthals, who were both musicians with the local symphony, were actively involved in the rehearsal, coaching their daughter through the session, offering suggestions about phrasing, tempo, and timing. "I couldn't believe what I was seeing and hearing. I was so envious that her parents knew what she was doing and cared about it. I wanted that family to be mine."

The meeting with the Lowenthals was a defining event in Kevin's musical life. It was not only his first face-to-face encounter with professional musicians, it was the first time he heard the sound of a solo cello. He was mesmerized. "It was incredible; I knew right away that I had to learn to play a stringed instrument."

A few weeks later, a neighbor heard about his wish and lent him a viola that had been lying unused in her attic. "I brought the viola home and was very nervous, very excited. It was like the first time you have sex with somebody; the anticipation was extreme."

But he was a pianist and had no idea what to do with the viola. With no other resources in the house to help him, he turned to the encyclopedia. "I thought I could find pictures of people playing so I could figure out which side it goes on and how you hold it. But I couldn't. I finally figured out how it worked without any help."

Soon he was playing the piano less and the viola more and begging for lessons. His parents, not knowing how to find a viola teacher, sought advice from Mrs. Lowenthal, who agreed to take him on herself. "From the first lesson, it was an entirely different experience from anything in my life up to that time. Now I had a teacher who talked about Beethoven and Mozart and serious classical music. And she was very demanding. She'd tell me I had the skill but not the discipline. But she also understood that I was alone in this, that I didn't have any help, so she was very encouraging. I studied with her for the next several years; she was a turning point in my musical life."

When he was fourteen years old, only one year after he began to play the viola, he auditioned for the Youth Symphony and won a seat. Suddenly, a whole new world opened before him. Until then, his life had been so distant from the world of musicians that, even in imagination, its outlines were shadowy and unsubstantial. Now it was real. "I was in this world with all these people my own age, all interested in classical music. There were fourteen violists, all like me. I never had such an experience before. The first time I played in the orchestra, a piece by Wagner, I felt like crying. My family wasn't even there; they didn't think it was important enough to come.

"That was the final breaking-off point with them. Whatever life I had with them before that ended, and a new life started. Out of my meeting with the Lowenthals, I had found the world of classical music and classical musicians, and I never looked back."

By the time he finished high school, Kevin was accomplished enough to win a scholarship to one of the most prestigious music conservatories in the country. There he studied with the woman he considers his teacher, the one he credits with the deepest level of his musical development. "I'll always be grateful to her. She gave me my career. She taught me how to play music, and she taught me how to teach as well.

"When I first started to study with her, she said that I had musical skills but that I was so walled up I was like one huge brick. I was fine technically, but I wasn't making music because the emotions were so blocked. She was the one who reached inside me and shook my emotions loose. She scared me; she made me work harder than anybody else has ever made me work. But she was also there for me to lean on while I sorted out the emotions inside me through my playing.

"I knew I'd achieved what we were looking for some time later when I played Bach's C Minor Cello Suite—the same piece I played for you—for her. I had worked very hard to identify the different emotions I wanted to express in the music—anger, screaming, pity, loneliness. My goal going into that lesson was to make her feel the music so deeply that she'd cry. I played it from memory with my eyes closed. My eyes teared up, and I opened them and saw that she was crying," he says, tears welling up once again as he remembers the moment. Then, pausing to gain control, he concludes, "When I play now, that's my goal, to give an audience insight into my emotions, my soul. And it's a very important part of what I teach."

Life in the conservatory was a revelation for Kevin. "I finally got to live in a place where people were like me. I was soaking it up, making up for all the time in high school and before that I wasn't exposed to music, art, literature, and intelligent conversation. But," he says sadly, "I had a lot of catching up to do. It was hard, a new experience for me. I'd always felt ahead of the people around me before; then all of a sudden, I was behind."

He tells of the time he sat listening to his lunch companions discuss Maria Callas's performance in *La Traviata* and felt bewildered and ashamed because he didn't know what they were talking about. "I didn't even know what *La Traviata* was." He tells of hearing fellow students, other string players, discuss Mendelssohn's quartets and feeling chagrined because he had never heard the music, didn't even know it existed. "As soon as I could get away, I went to the library and sat there for three hours listening to all the Mendelssohn string quartets."

As I listen to Kevin, I'm reminded of my own painful struggle to "catch up," to live in a world different from the one I knew in my childhood, to find comfort and belonging in a place where people always seemed to know about things I hadn't yet heard of. I grew up in a family where my mother, the only adult in the household, was an illiterate immigrant who never, even after many years in this country, learned to read or write. There wasn't a single book in our house; no one ever heard of classical music or had any interest in art; and the only question my mother had about the social and political events of the day was, "Is it good or bad for the Jews?"

The impoverishment of culture in my family notwithstanding, I was fortunate to grow up in New York City at a time when its school system was still intact and when its marvelous museums were open to the public free of charge. It was at school that I first heard a piece of classical music and sat enthralled by the sound. There, too, I was exposed to the wonders of the Metropolitan Museum of Art, to which my class was taken on a field trip. Later, as a teenager, I would go there to look at the pictures, hungering to be in the presence of the beauty I couldn't fully understand.

But these were small efforts of compensation, too small to overcome the many areas of ignorance wrought by my background and sustained by class and cultural norms that sent me to work instead of college immediately after my high school graduation. Consequently, as a young adult, I often cringed in humiliation when I listened to others talk about music I'd never heard, books I didn't know, ideas that were alien.

It made no difference that those others didn't realize my ignorance, that I was facile enough by then to cover it over. I knew, and that's what counted. Like Kevin, therefore, I set out to learn what I didn't know as fast as I could. If someone talked about a book I hadn't read, I was at the library the next day. If it was unfamiliar music that was under discussion, I sought it out as quickly as possible.

When, at thirty-nine, I became a freshman at the University of California at Berkeley, I had already spent many years trying to catch up. But despite my aptitude as a student, I never felt that I had closed the gap. Now, these many years later, I'm aware of how far I've come and also of how far I have yet to go—a distance that will, I fear, never be breached because I came so late to the world I now inhabit.

For Kevin, too, life has been a continuing effort to catch up. Although he feels competent professionally and prides himself on his musical knowledge and ability, he still has times when he feels like an impostor, moments of doubt when he walks out onto the stage and hears an inner voice warn, *"Watch it; be careful they don't find out."*

Socially, he says, he's on "constant alert," always aware that he might stumble into a situation or a conversation that will confront him with his ignorance. "Away from music, I still always feel there are holes and gaps. A few years ago, a new friend was talking about the sculptures of Bernini, and I thought, *Who?* I had to go to the library to find out he was one of the central figures of the Italian Renaissance," he says, his lips smiling but his eyes pained at the memory of his ignorance.

"When I'm at a party and people are talking about some esoteric subject, I'm taking notes in my head. *What are they talking about? What do I need to know so I can get into this conversation next time?* It doesn't have to be something so esoteric either. There are a lot of social things I don't know that other people take for granted, like which wine glass goes with which wine.

"It's hard sometimes, but I've gotten very good at using other people and their knowledge and experience to keep climbing up," he says. Then, fearful that his words might be misunderstood, he cautions, "It sounds opportunistic, but it's not what I mean. It's just that people can be resources of information and creativity, and I want to be able to learn from them. When someone knows something I don't know, it's a challenge. I want to know it.

"People like that, people who can teach you something, cross our paths frequently. The trick is to see them. All my life I've been able to identify those people and to gather what I need from them—their experience, their knowledge—to move along."

It wasn't just what Kevin didn't know that made him feel like an outsider in the social world; it was also what he *did* know. For Kevin McLaren is a gay man who knew he was "different" when he was eleven years old. When other boys talked about girls, dreamed about them, held them in the center of their masturbatory fantasies, he remained unmoved. "I just wasn't sexually attracted to women. I identified with them because I seemed to have more in common with the way women thought than with the way men thought about things. But I wasn't interested in women as sexual objects."

Like many gay men, however, his first sexual relationship was with a woman. "I dated in high school like everybody else. It was fine. But I think the real reason I did it was that having relationships with girls allowed me to get closer to men. By dating girls and sleeping with them, I became a part of the fraternity of men because I could talk about girls."

When Kevin was seventeen, he had his first homosexual experience. "It was with my best friend in high school, and it was very accidental. I think he was curious, but for me it was lust. He asked me to touch him, and I did. And then the touching extended beyond just that. That was my first time, but it was really more my pleasuring him.

"It wasn't until I went to the conservatory and was away from home and my parents that I really felt the freedom to explore my sexuality. There, I found lots of people who were willing to help me do that. Before that time, I'd think that I probably was gay, but that I could get away with not being gay. After that, I knew I was gay."

His parents' response to his coming out surprised him at first. "It all seemed so casual. I was living with this man, Don, at the time, but I had never said what my relationship with him was. Then, one day when I was visiting my parents, my father just came out and asked if he was my lover. I said yes. He very calmly said, 'Maybe we should include your mother in talking about this.' So he called her in and told her I'd said I was gay. She asked, 'Are you gay or bisexual?' I told her I'd come to terms with being gay. She was very relaxed about it and just said something about worrying about my health and discrimination in my professional life. It was all very matter-of-fact.

"But as usual in my family, there was a lot going on below the surface. At Christmas a couple of months later, we all met at my sister's house. It was the first time my parents saw me and Don together like that. It was a perfectly pleasant visit, but I remember thinking, 'This is too easy.' And I was right. A couple of weeks later, my sister called to tell me that my mother was in the hospital. She had plunged into a depression after that manic Christmas and tried to kill my father. That's the way my mother could express her rage and disappointment. It was the real beginning of my parents confronting my being gay."

The road to a satisfying personal life, a life that included the kind of stable, intimate relationship he yearned for, hasn't been easy. "The first long-term relationship I had was when I was twenty and he was the same age. It was like pretending to be grownups. I don't know, maybe it's particular to gay men. You want to create a relationship that emulates society's definition of a loving relationship. So we did all those things. We went to Sears and bought dishes; we had two cats; we played house. But there was no really common bond and no communication except for music, which wasn't enough. So it ended."

Soon after, he got involved with a man who was nine years older than he but who, he says, was more his intellectual equal. "We could talk about philosophy and architecture and the kind of intellectual topics I was interested in. But with all that, it was a relationship that most resembled the one my parents had—big arguments followed by happy times followed by big arguments." A year and a half after it started, the relationship collapsed when his lover unceremoniously announced it was over. It was a devastating experience for Kevin, one that left him reeling. "It was the lowest point of my life," he recalls. "I felt terrible about myself."

Until then, he had never lived alone, having lived either in his parents' home, in a campus dormitory, or in an apartment with a roommate or lover. Now, for the first time, he was totally alone. Lonely and frightened, he stepped back, surveyed his life, and determined to change it. "It was a transforming experience for me because I had no distractions. I had to confront myself and my past in a whole new way. It was like slapping myself in the face and saying, 'Okay, so it hurts; now grow up and take responsibility for your life.'

"I lived alone for four years. During that time, I trimmed off the dead branches of my life. It was like wiping off a cloudy glass so I could see what was real inside. I came out of that with a closer relationship to my creativity, which is the thing that has always been my life preserver. When I was a very little child and my parents would fight, I would draw. Later, when I had the piano, I'd practice. When I didn't have friends and felt alone, I would go to my music. Always I could go inside myself and create something."

Today, many of Kevin McLaren's dreams have come true. Professionally, his life is flourishing as he makes his mark both as a concert artist and a professor of music. "It took a while to learn that it wasn't about people telling me I was special and had these great gifts. I had to work hard and prove it, and I did."

Personally, he has lived for five years with Peter Crawford, a highly educated, urbane man more than twenty years his senior. "Part of my initial attraction to Peter was his experience and his maturity. I've learned a lot from him; I'm still learning," he says. Then, his eyes alight as he speaks about the relationship, he adds, "That's not all, of course; we're great together. I've never had the kind of intimacy and communication we have. It's what I've always wanted."

His relationship with his sister, Susan, has grown and changed so that they now have a warm friendship. "I think we've finally worked out the rivalry that separated us, and it gives me a sense of security to know she's there. There's a sense of identification because we shared a life that I don't feel with anyone else."

But he worries about her. Although Susan is married and has children and a successful professional life, she never fully separated from the family and its pathology. "She always had trouble knowing the boundaries between them and her, and she was always more reactive to them and that environment than I was," Kevin says sadly. "She couldn't really make the kind of distance that was necessary to survive. So she'd interpret their crazy actions very personally, as if they were aimed at her or they were her fault. They can still hook her into the family drama."

Now, in her mid-thirties, Susan shows evidence of the same manic-depressive illness that felled her mother—the same extreme mood swings from depression to mania and all the symptoms that attend them. "I was lucky," Kevin says; "I was spared."

Since this is one of the few psychological illnesses that we know is hereditary, the luck of the genes may, indeed, account for some of the difference between Susan and Kevin. But the differences in how they handled the family pathology—his disidentification, his ability to stand separate from them, his capacity to know that what he calls "their craziness" had nothing to do with him—also account for the fact that he was "spared."

His parents' lives continue much as they were when he was a child, except that the violence between them has grown worse in recent years. A month or two before we met, his father responded to his mother's manic episode by trying to control her physically. No one knows exactly what happened or who was actually threatening whom. But Katherine McLaren called the police who, seeing the bruises on her arms, took her husband into custody and charged him with assault. Eventually, Mrs. McLaren wound up in the hospital again, and the charges against her husband were dropped. But not until the drama had played itself out in the family.

Responding to my question about how he feels about these events, Kevin says calmly, "The first time I got one of those calls, I put the phone down and sobbed uncontrollably. I felt profound grief inside, like my parents were dead and all that was left was these two people living together in this sick, dysfunctional relationship. But then you get used to it; you have to. So this time when my sister called to tell me the story, I felt like we were talking about people we know, not about our parents."

It isn't that he has rejected his parents or that he has no relationship with them. He speaks with them regularly and visits when he can. But it's no different from when he was a child. He knew then and he knows now that there's nothing he can do to change their lives. "I wish it were different, but this is their life, and there's nothing I can do about it."

And he knows, too, that however hard they may try, they're incapable of understanding his life or the world he lives in. "When I was at the conservatory, my parents came to two recitals, one I gave in my freshman year, one in my senior year. From that time on, they didn't hear me play until about twelve years later, when I twisted their arm to come hear me play a concerto with an orchestra."

He stops speaking for a few minutes; then, his words angry but his eyes filled with pain, he continues, "After the performance they came backstage and looked stricken. My father looked ill; my mother looked like she was going to cry. And they both kept shaking their heads as if they couldn't understand what they were witnessing. Seeing me getting all that applause and respect was incomprehensible to them. It was as if I were a total stranger. I couldn't tell whether they were proud or pained."

The reality, of course, is that he is a total stranger to them, just as they are to him. For Kevin, whatever sadness he feels is mitigated by his triumph in the distance he's come. It's proof that he succeeded in his determination to make a life that's different from theirs, evidence of the talent that helped him to do so. His parents, however, could only listen to the applause with a combination of pride and pain—pride in this son they don't really know, pain as they understood perhaps more clearly than ever just how much of a stranger he had become.

eight

Karen Richards:
The Child Who Was Sold

THE LATE AUGUST SUN IS ALREADY BEGINNING TO LOSE SOME OF ITS summer warmth as seven-year-old Kaarina Juusonen and her mother approach the docks in Göteborg, Sweden. Kaarina, a thin, wiry child, small for her age, holds tightly to her mother's hand as they make their way through the milling throng and head for the pier where a large ocean liner is preparing to embark.

The journey from the Juusonen's home in Finland was long and tiresome, but Kaarina perks up excitedly as they near the ship. Her mother, Marianne, had told her she was going to America where she'd never be hungry again and would have as many new dresses and toys as she wanted. So in her child's mind, Kaarina imagines a huge store whose shelves are stocked with all the things her impoverished family can't afford. The ship, she thinks, must be America.

When they reach the vessel, Marianne stops to speak to a uniformed stranger who disengages Kaarina from her mother and leads her up the gangplank. She strains at the man's hand, looking back toward her mother who remains on the dock, her hand raised in a gesture of farewell. Before Kaarina can grasp what has happened, she's alone on the deck of the ship as it weighs anchor and edges away from its berth. She runs to the side, hoping she'll see her mother climbing aboard. But she's too small to see over the top. Frantically, she pulls herself up until she can wedge her face between the steel uprights that support the ship's rail and watches as her mother becomes a small dot in the sea of people who remain on the shore. Trembling with fear, she calls out, "Mama, mama, please, I don't want to go." But there's no one to hear her plea.

As the ship picks up speed and the shoreline recedes, she looks around bewildered. The deck is crowded with people waving good-bye to friends and loved ones, chattering excitedly about the voyage that lies ahead. Kaarina closes her eyes, squeezing them tight in a child's magical hope that if she can't see it, it will all go away. But she's still there, alone and frightened, when she opens them again. She sinks down onto the deck and huddles against the bulwark, tears coursing silently down her cheeks and staining the little flowered dress her grandmother had made for her and that, just moments earlier, she had tended with such care and pride.

Soon the other passengers go off to their cabins to settle in for the journey while she remains in place, a small almost invisible bundle of fear. *Where am I going? Why is she sending me away? What did I do?* She doesn't know how long she sits there, her mind racing wildly, before a ship's attendant finds her and escorts her to the tiny cabin where she'll spend the next half-dozen days so wretchedly seasick she's barely able to move.

Today, little Kaarina has become Karen Richards, a still small, still wiry, fifty-year-old woman who was referred to me for psychotherapy some years ago. "She's a very appealing woman; I think you'll find her quite interesting," the colleague who referred her said, as she sketched for me the outlines of Karen's harrowing past and warned also that she probably would be a "tough case." But nothing prepared me for the tale of abandonment and cruelty that marked Karen's childhood and adolescence. Nor for the immediate connection I made with her, a connection so profound that I often found myself feeling her feelings and anticipating her words.

It's not unusual, of course, for a therapist to feel connected to a patient. Indeed, such a connection is essential to the success of the therapeutic endeavor. Without it, there can be no relationship, and without a relationship, there is no therapy. But there was something different about my response to Karen, something I couldn't name at the time but that seemed related more to who she was than to anything I brought to our encounters.

It wasn't until I began to do the research for this book and reflect on what I was learning that I understood that part of what drew me so powerfully to her was the same quality of adoptability I have spoken of so frequently here. Like the others who triumphed over the trials of their past, Karen Richards has the ability not only to attract people who can help erase the deficits left by the past but to use well what others can offer.

It's this capacity that she brought to the therapeutic setting—this, plus a well-honed intelligence, the ability to do psychological work that would enliven any therapist's heart, and an absolute refusal to engage in self-pity or to see herself as a victim—that made her so attractive and engaged me so deeply. When, for example, I asked if she would be willing to tell her story for this book, she thought about it for a few days, then agreed saying, "The only reason I hesitated is because I can't stand people who go around complaining about their lives, and I don't want to sound like one of them. I hate this whole thing these days where everyone feels like a victim. I've had some hard times, but I'm not a victim."

Now, as we begin the interview and I listen once again to the story of her voyage to America and the chamber of horrors she entered from the day her mother abandoned her on the ship, I feel the same pull I have always felt in her presence and the same sense of awe at the resilience of the human spirit. "Vomit and fear, that's what stands out about that trip," she says, her angry words striking the air like a whip. "I was alone in that little room for the whole crossing, and I was throwing up all the time. For some reason, they brought my food to me in the cabin, so I always ate there alone. The only other time I saw anyone was when they came to change the bed or wash me.

"Everything I had with me was in this little pressed cardboard suitcase not much bigger than a woman's handbag: one dress, a pair of underpants, a pair of long pants, a shirt, two tiny copper coffee pots—gifts for the people in America—and a little wooden airplane my brother had made. Since I had so few clothes and I was throwing up so much, someone had to keep washing them."

Complicating an already terrifying experience, the ship and its staff were Swedish, and Kaarina spoke only Finnish. So although some of the people who tended her might have wanted to be kind, there was no way to communicate across the language barrier. For six long days and nights, Kaarina lived in terror, her voice stilled, her mind numbed by shock. "I couldn't understand what was happening or why, and I couldn't even speak to anyone. It was like living in a nightmare. I'd never been alone before. I was so scared; I kept screaming for *aiti*, which is the Finnish word for mother. I've totally forgotten the Finnish language; it's as if I never spoke it. But that's the one word I never forgot—*aiti*.

"Until the boat left without her, I thought my mother was coming to this America with me. In fact, when I saw the boat, I thought it *was* America because America as a country was totally beyond my understanding. What I understood was that I would be able to get clothes and toys and have enough food to eat, then we'd come back home and I'd show my brothers the things I got. I didn't get it until I actually got to America. And it didn't penetrate until I'd been in America for a very long time that I wasn't going back home."

She stops speaking as tears spring to her eyes. "Dammit, it was so long ago, I don't want to be crying over all that anymore," she says, shaking herself impatiently. Then, her voice crackling with emotion, she asks, "How does a mother do that to a child? She sold me for a couple of bottles of booze, a few packs of cigarettes, some coffee, and a new dress."

Karen was born in 1944, shortly before the end of World War II, a war that caused havoc in Finland, as it had elsewhere in Europe. Poverty was rampant, tuberculosis epidemic. Her father, who had spent most of his adult life in a TB sanitarium, died before her first birthday, leaving his thirty-three-year-old wife with three children and no skills.

Her mother, Marianne Juusonen, was never much of a caretaker, even when her husband was alive. Long before Kaarina was born, Marianne had served a prison term for negligent child endangerment, a conviction that grew out of the mysterious death of her three-year-old daughter, who either fell or was pushed out of an upper-story window.

Except for brief stints as a cleaning woman, Marianne was unemployed, largely because, with her husband's death, she became increasingly sunk in alcoholism. "I don't have a lot of memories of my mother's house. But when I think about it, I remember a lot of hollering and all kinds of violent noises. Her whole personality changed when she drank. She'd get very loud, and there'd be all this fighting. To this day, I'm never around alcoholics; I've simply chosen not to be around people who drink," says Karen, her face a mask of distaste.

"My brother and I used to go to the bars, sometimes at midnight, looking for her. We'd stand outside looking in, waiting for her to come home. Sometimes she'd come out with some man and bring him home; sometimes she'd be alone."

As her memories surface, Karen turns pale, her mind returning to a scene she wants to forget. "There were bottles on the bureau," she says, as if to distract herself. At the mention of the bottles, however, her composure fades, and she seems to become three years old again—a tired child lying on her cot, listening to the raucous laughter of her mother and a companion who had been drinking heavily for some time. She twists and turns, trying unsuccessfully to shut out the sounds they make. Finally, their voices are stilled, and she relaxes into the quiet.

But before Kaarina can drift off to sleep, the man stumbles up to her bed and pulls her out of it. She stands there for a moment shivering in her thin nightdress, then frightened, begins to back away. But the room is small, and she soon finds herself backed up against the bureau. As he comes toward her, she takes another step backward, and with it, knocks the bottles to the floor. He grabs her, his breath reeking from alcohol, his rough clothes scratching her face. She screams for her mother, but Marianne doesn't respond.

"I don't remember exactly what happened after that," says Karen, "only that I felt like I was being smothered, like there was a gun in my throat. I screamed and screamed, but my mother never came. She was there, but she never came."

With these words, she seems to return to her adult self. Then, pushing her hair back in a characteristic gesture that signals her distress, she says, "The worst part of thinking about that isn't the sexual abuse. So many terrifying things happened to me later—like being alone on that ship and the life I had when I came here—that the sexual abuse itself doesn't seem of primary importance. What feels so terrible to me is that my mother was there, and she let it happen; she didn't come to protect me."

But for protection little Kaarina could look only to her older brother, who was confined to a tuberculosis hospital much of the time; or to her grandmother, Marianne's mother, who was a stern woman, undemonstrative in what Karen describes as "that typical Finnish way." Nevertheless, she was there for the child, feeding her, sewing the few clothes she owned, allowing her to participate in the small chores of daily life, providing the stability her mother could not. "I don't know where my mother was; she didn't work most of the time. She just wasn't very good at taking care of us; she liked her liquor and her fun.

"I think I'd usually go home to sleep at night. But during the day, I was mostly with my grandmother. Like I said, she didn't show affection, but I think she cared for me. One of the few good memories I have of those days is of my grandmother's room. She lived in this sunny, corner room, and she had geraniums on the window sills," she recalls, her face lighting in a smile as her memory takes her back to that room.

She stops speaking, lost in thought for a few moments, then looks up and, shaking her head in puzzlement, sighs, "It's a paradox, isn't it? I don't really have any mental picture of my grandmother. I can see her room but not her. The image I carry around is of my mother, yet it was my grandmother who would feed me and take care of me. My mother never even cooked unless it was some type of oatmeal and weak coffee."

A few months before Kaarina's seventh birthday, her mother was solicited by an American lawyer of Finnish extraction who was looking for children to place with American families. No one will ever know why Marianne Juusonen agreed to sell her daughter or how much she got for her, although it's a fair guess that it wasn't much. Whatever her more venal motives, however, it's reasonable to assume that she also really believed—or at least rationalized the decision sufficiently to convince herself—that she was sending her daughter to a better life. All we know for sure is that soon after the offer was made, little Kaarina Juusonen found herself alone on an ocean liner bound for America.

After what seemed an interminable journey, she arrived in New York to be met by Vivian Thompson, the lawyer who had arranged for her adoption, and her husband, Richard. Shaken from the voyage, dazed, and disoriented, Karen disembarked into a world she couldn't have imagined. "I was seven years old and had never even been sent to school. I did know how to read; somehow I learned to do that. But my comprehension of the world was very limited. We lived on the outskirts of Helsinki, right on the edge of the forest, and were excruciatingly poor. That was my world. I'd never even been in a private car before I came to America.

"When I got off the ship in New York, I couldn't believe it. Everything looked overwhelmingly big," she recalls, her arms spread wide to describe the scene that greeted her. "And the smell, the air reeked from diesel fumes. To this day when I smell those fumes I remember that moment."

Perhaps because she was so determined that no one would take her mother's place, perhaps because she had a premonition of things to come, Kaarina had an immediate aversive response to Vivian Thompson. "This man and woman were standing side by side. I'm not sure, but I have the feeling that the woman made a gesture toward me, like putting her hands out, but I remember looking at her face, and something I saw there frightened me. She spoke Finnish, so she was the one person I could talk to when I arrived. But even so, I knew the minute I looked at her that I didn't like her. So I went to the man instead. He smiled and picked me up and gave me a doll.

"That was the beginning of my trouble with Vivian Thompson who, it turned out, was going to adopt me. The family that was supposed to adopt me changed their minds before the papers became final because they were leery of taking a seven-year-old. Vivian could have stopped the whole thing, but unfortunately, she didn't, so I ended up with her.

"I didn't know any of that then, of course. I didn't know anything, certainly not what I was doing there. And I didn't have any idea that she would be my new mother. I had a mother, and it didn't occur to me there'd be another one," she says, her voice rising in indignation as she recalls the bewilderment of that seven-year-old child.

For Kaarina, the journey to the small midwestern town, where Vivian Thompson had a successful law practice and was a powerful force in the community, was a continuation of the nightmare she had been living since the ship she sailed on left port. Dick Thompson tried to be kind, but Vivian, the only one to whom she could make herself understood, had little patience with the child's pain. "I could tell right away I was a bother to her."

When they arrived in what would be her home, Kaarina, by then renamed Karen, was introduced to her new family—the Thompson's biological son, Ezra, who was three years younger than she; Vivian's eight siblings and their children; and Vivian's mother. "They seemed nice enough, but I felt like I was in a circus or something," recalls Karen.

Like Petar Steprovic, who also suffered a name change, Karen loathed her new name. *"Karen!"* she says, the word exploding off her tongue like an expletive. "It wasn't my name. I didn't know the person that name belonged to. I hated the sound of it then, and I still don't like it. Kaarina has nice soft sounds, not like Karen; it sounds hard," she says, as she sounds out the Finnish and English versions of her name to demonstrate the difference.

But it wasn't just the sound of her new name from which Kaarina/ Karen recoiled, it was from the new identity that went with it, an identity that signaled the obliteration of her old life for which she longed so intensely. For her, too, accepting the new name was made more difficult because, she says, "It was given to me by a person I grew to hate and fear, yet who I was dependent on. For as long as I can remember, I dreaded knowing that my name might be called because when she noticed me, it meant trouble. I used to walk very quietly; I closed doors quietly; I didn't want to breathe so as not to call attention to myself."

Distressed and disoriented as she was when she arrived, Karen didn't lose the capacity to capture someone's heart and to seek comfort in a relationship—in this case, Vivian Thompson's mother, a Finnish immigrant who was a reminder of the grandmother she left behind. "She was kind to me from the beginning, so I glommed onto her. Later on, I'd go there after school, and she'd feed me. She read

Finnish newspapers like my grandmother did, and I'd sit there with her and we'd read the newspapers like I used to do with my grandmother. Sometimes I stayed at her house, and then she'd let me sleep in her bed, right next to her."

In the Thompson household, however, there was no such comfort. There, Karen's life was driven by Vivian's cruelty almost from the day she arrived. I listen to the details with wonder, trying to figure out why Vivian Thompson would have adopted the child when she had so little tolerance for her. Although the answer eludes me, one thing is clear: Despite her capacity to function well in her social and professional world, Vivian was capable of behavior that can only be described as psychotic—a psychosis that became nucleated around Karen. It was as if the child's presence threw Vivian into a psychotic rage that could be satisfied only by perpetrating sometimes unimaginable horrors upon her. "Everybody knew—her husband, my teachers, my aunts and uncles, the doctors, even the pastor of the church. But nobody ever intervened to stop her. She was prominent in the community, had political clout in Washington, and was the most powerful person in the family. Who was I going to complain to?" Karen asks bitterly. "The few times I did, I was met with deaf ears.

"Dick Thompson tried to be nice to me, but he couldn't stop her. Nobody could; they were all too afraid of her. They felt sorry for me, but I hated the pity I saw in their eyes and the way they looked away so their eyes wouldn't have to meet mine.

"She was my own personal torturer, my own personal trainer into the terrors of a relationship," Karen observes, as she describes the savagery of the humiliations and the beatings she endured. "She'd do things like drag me to school and make me stand in front of the class and declare that I was a worthless guttersnipe. *Guttersnipe*, that was one of her favorite words for me."

And pain. For Karen, the word is synonymous with her adoptive mother. "The earliest physical pain I remember came from Vivian Thompson—the beatings, the kicks in the ribs, the whacks on the legs, the hair pullings, the belt, the Ping-Pong paddle." Those were the constants, the stuff of Karen's daily life.

Then there were the special events: "There are so many things, so much cruelty and pain, day and night. It got so I was afraid to be awake and afraid to go to sleep. That was maybe the worst of all; I had to be vigilant all the time, always prepared for the attack."

Normally, Karen Richards speaks spontaneously in a voice that registers a wide range of emotions. But as she recounts her suffering at the hands of her adoptive mother, she becomes unnaturally contained, her voice flat, the play of expression usually visible on her face blanked out. As I watch the change come over her, I'm puzzled at first. I had, after all, heard some of these stories before in my role as therapist and was always impressed with the appropriateness of the affect she brought to the room. *Why now does she suddenly seem wooden?* I wonder.

It's only after I've listened for awhile that I begin to understand. It was one thing to tell her tale piecemeal, part of it in one session, another perhaps weeks later when the emotional fallout from the first had been dealt with. It raises quite another set of feelings to tell it all at once, one terrible experience following another, as an interview requires. Then, the only way to avoid being overwhelmed by the memory of her suffering is to numb herself during the telling.

She sits very quietly, therefore, her voice calm as she tells about the pots of boiling water Vivian threw at her when her rage went out of control; about the many times she pushed her into a closet and locked her into the cramped darkness for hours; about the wooden hoe that would come crashing down on her back when she was weeding and that once hit so hard that it cracked a vertebrae; about being dragged out of bed in the middle of the night and made to scrub the kitchen floor; about the hours when she was forced to sit upright in a chair while she was abused both verbally and physically; about the day Vivian came after her with a scissors as she cowered on the floor, pulled her upright by her ponytail, and furiously chopped her hair off so close to the scalp that she bled; about the time Vivian dumped her head into a toilet full of vomit.

"That may have been the worst," says Karen, "because it happened right after I came, before I had any idea what to expect. I was only here a week or so and had just started school, and I couldn't understand a word of what was going on. That morning I was so upset and scared about having to go there that I couldn't keep my breakfast down. So I ran to the toilet and vomited. She followed me screaming about what a mess and a sad sack I was. That was another one of her favorite words for me, *sad sack,*" she adds parenthetically. "Then, before I could get up off my knees, she grabbed me by my ponytail and pushed my whole head, hair and all, down into the toilet. She kept doing that over and over again, pulling my head up by my ponytail and then pushing it down into the toilet. My head kept banging into the bowl until I thought I'd pass out. To this day, I don't know how I didn't.

"When she finally stopped, I was soaked from head to foot. She stripped off my clothes, which were full of vomit, and threw me into the shower to rinse off. She let me put on dry clothes, but she wouldn't let me wash the vomit out of my hair or off my shoes. That's the way she made me go to school, stinking from vomit."

As she tells this story, her reserve finally breaks down, her eyes flash with fury, her face twists into a mask of pain. "It's hard to believe, isn't it? But believe me when I tell you it's only the tip of the iceberg."

In this atmosphere, it's no surprise that all Karen could think of was her mother and her home in Finland. Vivian, however, was determined to wipe all memory from the child's mind. When she cried for her mother, Vivian warned that if she didn't stop, she'd give her "something to cry about." When she asked when she'd be going home, Vivian snarled, "Never. Nobody there wants you anymore; that's why they sent you away." When she spoke Finnish, Vivian mocked and slapped her.

But even then, even when she was at her most vulnerable, Karen refused to surrender total control to her tormentor. Instead, in what was soon to become her characteristic way of dealing with the abuse that was visited upon her, she retreated inside, to her own secret place in her mind where she kept the memories that sustained her. "When I first came, she took away everything I brought with me, even the little wooden airplane my brother had given me. There was no safe place for anything that was mine in that house, not even my memories. So I made a little black box in my mind. It was my memory box, and I kept my things in it—my grandmother's room, the geraniums on her windowsill, my brother Lars, and my mother, mostly my mother. I remember literally putting my mother's image in the box for safekeeping, and every night, when Vivian Thompson couldn't see me, I'd pick up the lid and look at it."

Despite Vivian's insistence that she had been thrown away by her family, Karen clung to the belief that someone would come for her some day. "I was devastated when she'd say those things, but in an odd way, I also never really believed it. I kept thinking that someone from my family would come and get me and show her she was wrong and that they did care about me." She pauses, as the memory brings tears to her eyes, and adds ruefully, "I guess I had to believe that to survive what she did to me."

Still, the degradation and brutality she suffered at Vivian's hands— the contemptuous reminders that she was worthless, the endlessly inventive ways of humiliating her, the merciless physical cruelty— took their toll. "I felt like a geek and a freak, like I was a disgusting nonentity, especially during my teenage years. The loneliness was unbearable, and so was the sense of being so different.

"I spent a lot of time trying to figure out what was wrong with me, but I couldn't ever figure it out. The closest I came was thinking it had something to do with some shameful thing about me and my family back in Finland that Vivian Thompson knew about."

But while her adoptive mother's hatred obviously affected her sense of herself, there was also a side of Karen that stood in powerful opposition to her—the side that refused to accept wholly the degraded image Vivian pressed upon her so insistently, the side that never fully surrendered herself, the side that found ways to fight back. "If there's one word to describe how I got by, it would be *defiance*. She wanted to break me, and I wouldn't let her," Karen says, her expression a mixture of revulsion and triumph.

Sometimes the defiance was covert, a hidden act that she could hold to herself in secret retaliation. "For most of the years I lived in that house, I wasn't allowed to eat with the family because she said I didn't deserve to sit at the table with decent people. So I'd be eating in the kitchen and she'd be ordering me around in her nasty, angry voice, 'Bring this to the table, Madam; bring that to the table, and hurry up about it.' Nobody else said anything. Dick Thompson would sit there with a face like a stone mask, and my brothers just looked confused. So sometimes I'd get so mad that I'd spit in the food before I carried it out to them."

Sometimes her defiance was more overt, as when she refused to cry no matter how much physical pain and humiliation she had to bear. It wasn't unusual for Vivian to pull her out of bed by her hair at two or three o'clock in the morning and drag her down to the kitchen, where she forced her to her knees and made her scrub the floor, all the while hitting and kicking her because she wasn't doing it well enough or fast enough. "No matter what she did, I just kept washing the floor; I wouldn't let her see me cry."

Or Vivian would push Karen into a chair and refuse to allow her to move until she recited some prescribed words. Sometimes it was an apology for a crime the child knew she hadn't committed; sometimes it was a demand that she agree to her unworthiness. But no matter how long Vivian made her sit there, no matter how hard the blows that rained down on her, Karen refused to acquiesce and speak the required words.

Undoubtedly, such resistance made things worse for her, since it enraged her adoptive mother further and was evidence, in Vivian's warped mind, that the child was incorrigible. But in refusing to bend totally to the demands of her oppressor, Karen preserved her integrity and with it, her sanity.

As the torture persisted, Karen developed the capacity to remove herself psychologically even while her body remained in place. "I was about nine years old the first time it happened. It was one of those times when she made me sit in a chair until I said whatever it was she wanted me to say. But I was damned if I would say it. She'd come by and hit me or pull my hair or spit on me, and I remember my body sitting in the chair but my mind left. I just tuned out everything she said and did. At first, it was like I was floating above it all, watching everything going on around me. I could see them all, but I wasn't there. But then it changed. It was like I went into this very long, dark tunnel where I could look out if I wanted to, but nothing could reach me.

"After awhile, I found I could recapture that experience almost at will, and I started to do it more and more when I was around her. Terrible things might be going on in the outside world, but I was safe, even though I was sitting right in the middle of it. Someone could have beaten me to a pulp when I was in there, and I don't think I would have felt it."

This kind of split between mind and body—what psychologists call *depersonalization*—is not an uncommon defense in the face of torture. But it can be a dangerous one, since it's often hard to come out of the tunnel—to bring the body and mind back together again—when there's no longer any reason to sustain the division. Indeed, torture victims who once escaped into their version of Karen's tunnel often can't be convinced to give it up, since it's the place that represents safety and freedom from pain.

Remarkably, when, even as a still defenseless child, Karen began to understand the seduction of her tunnel and its potential danger, she walked away from it and never went back. "I escaped into that tunnel for years. After a while, though, I became afraid of it. I was being sucked into it more and more, and I sensed it was dangerous. I began to be afraid that I wouldn't be able to come out when I wanted to, so I stopped letting myself do it."

When Karen was nearly twelve years old, the family adopted another Finnish child, this time a one-and-a-half-year-old boy. Whereas others who have been abused often become abusers, Karen moved quickly to the child's side, becoming his caretaker and protector and often taking upon herself the blows that might otherwise have gone to him. "I couldn't stand the idea that she might hurt him like she hurt me," is all she can say to explain her behavior. In fact, although Vivian apparently was incapable of real kindness to a child, and Benjamin got his share of punishments and beatings, she never abused him as viciously as she did Karen.

It wasn't just Karen's abhorrence of the violence she anticipated—although that undoubtedly was deeply felt—that moved her to champion Benjamin. It was also as if she understood intuitively—just as a parent who was abused in childhood often does—that in protecting Benjamin, in helping him to have a different experience, she could take a step toward healing the damaged child inside her.

In my own life, I remember the many times I felt as if I were holding myself when I held and comforted my daughter, giving to her what my mother could never give to me. It wasn't always easy to be the giving parent; I sometimes even envied my child her mother, wishing just once that I had felt the kind of safety I was able to provide for her. But most of the time, I could be what she needed, not just because I loved her but also because I understood in some deep but, at the time, inarticulate way that I could heal the pain of the past only if I succeeded in changing the present.

For Karen, it was somewhat different; she wasn't Benjamin's mother. But her relationship with him was, nevertheless, important both in her developing definition of herself and in helping her to withstand Vivian's assaults. Caring for Benjamin gave Karen's life a purpose that had been missing before he became part of the family. Until then, she was often despairing, wondering whether she could survive, sometimes whether she wanted to. After he arrived, when Vivian struck, she could remind herself that she couldn't give way to despair because Benjamin needed her. At the same time, with him she found the only love and warmth she knew in that icy household, an experience that not only nourished her spirit but affirmed for her that, despite Vivian's often-voiced judgment to the contrary, she was capable of sustaining a loving relationship.

When Karen was fifteen, Vivian finally did the unthinkable: She tried to push Karen out of a second-story window. "She actually tried to kill me. I always knew it was possible; so did other people. One of my great uncles even once told me he was afraid she'd kill me if I didn't get away from her. Not that he or anyone else ever offered to help," Karen says bitterly.

She stops talking and sits straighter in her chair, as if to brace herself for the story she has to tell. After a long silence, she speaks again. "I was cleaning the windows, sitting on the sill with my body half out, and she came along and began to holler that I had missed some spots. Then all of a sudden, she lunged at me and tried to push me out. I saw her coming and braced myself and caught the edge of the window and pushed back with all my strength. Finally, I was able to push her away so I could crawl out. There was a broom standing nearby, and I grabbed it and held it out in front of me and screamed at her, 'Don't you ever touch me again.' I meant it; I wanted to kill her, and she knew it. She never hit me again. I couldn't believe it; for the first time, I actually felt powerful," she concludes, the combination of rage and triumph she felt then palpable in the room.

Although the beatings stopped, the humiliations continued unabated, and Karen's inner life was dominated by dreams of escape. Her hatred of Karen notwithstanding, Vivian would not make it easy for her to leave. Thus, while the Thompsons were an upper middle-class family with plenty of money to support a child through college, Vivian was unwilling to offer her daughter any financial help at all. After graduating from high school, therefore, Karen continued to live at home, working at a clerical job all day, taking classes at a local college at night, and looking for a way out of the house.

It wasn't long after she started college that her opportunity came when she was befriended by Joan Gilman, a divorcee with two children who spoke of her problems in getting child care. "I thought I saw a way to break out," Karen recalls. "She knew Vivian Thompson; everybody in town did. But I knew she liked me, so I took a chance and told her very briefly what it was like for me in that house, and she asked me to come and live with her in exchange for some baby-sitting.

"I knew there would be a terrible scene when I told Vivian I was going to move out. So it took six months and every bit of courage I had to tell her. As I expected, she was incredibly violently angry. She told me never to darken her door again. But by then she couldn't get to me anymore."

Karen lived with her friend for several years in an arrangement that seems clearly to have come into being as much out of Joan's liking and concern for Karen as her usefulness as a baby-sitter, although she did her share of that. Meanwhile, she continued to work at her office job and finished college. Soon after her graduation, she moved to a nearby large city, where she got a job as a teacher.

In contrast to the terrible loneliness of her adolescent years, once Karen was out from under Vivian's domination, she found she could make friends easily and relax with them into the large and small pleasures of daily life. "When I left Vivian Thompson's house, I actually reinvented myself. I felt like I'd been released from hell, and I made up my mind to put all that behind me and enjoy my life. And I did. I made lots of friends, and they even called me by a different name: *Karey*.

"The years with my friend Joan were wonderful. Then when I left the town I grew up in, things took another big step forward. I had a job I liked; I found good friends, and I was having lots of fun. It was a great time."

Soon, however, she grew restless, wanting to explore more of the world than her life allowed. At twenty-four, therefore, she joined the Peace Corps and was sent to Venezuela. When her tour of duty was over two years later, she decided to visit a friend in California. "I never went back to the Midwest to live again," Karen says.

Since she didn't have a California teaching credential, she was faced with going back to school for a year to get one or taking an office job. She chose the latter. "I didn't have the money to get my credential, and besides, I was tired of working all day and going to school all night," she says.

Within a year after she moved West, she met and married her first husband—an artist who she describes as "very brilliant, very handsome, and very crazy." Six months later they separated.

Not long after her divorce, she became involved with Craig Marshall, the man who would become her daughter's father. "I never intended to marry him," she says, "but I got pregnant. It was a pregnancy that shouldn't have happened because he'd had a vasectomy. But it did, and then I had a big decision to make."

Given her past, it's not surprising that Karen had decided that she'd never have any children. "I was afraid I had bad blood, like I was genetically damaged," she explains, "and that I might become a mother like my own mother. Then, too, one of my worst fears was that I might die if I had a child. I couldn't bear the thought of leaving a child motherless like I was."

What we decide in the abstract, however, and what we do when faced with the reality often are different. After a trying period of indecision, she decided against an abortion and married Craig. Three years later they, too, separated. Only this time, when Karen went her own way, she took her daughter, Jennifer, with her. "I liked and admired him tremendously, but I was never in love with him," she explains now.

"The end came when I knew he was seeing other women and faced him with that. He became very angry and put his hands around my throat. He didn't really hurt me, and I was able to get away from him immediately. But I abhor physical violence, and that one violent act was enough. I packed up and took Jennifer and went to a friend's house." She pauses for a moment, then says thoughtfully, "I don't know. Maybe it was the excuse I needed, but I'd had enough violence in my life."

For the next several years, her life centered around Jennifer, with whom she had a close and loving relationship. As time passed, however, she grew increasingly bored and restless with her office job. She knew she'd eventually go back to school. But to do what? "The question was, was I going to get my California teaching credential, would I become a gardener in the city's parks, or would I go to law school."

Law school won—an interesting example, perhaps, of the way both identification and *dis*identification can coexist. On the one hand, Karen disidentified with her adoptive mother, even refusing ever to address her as *mother*. But at the same time, Vivian Thompson was, as Karen now acknowledges, "the only mother I ever really knew." It's no surprise, therefore, that the child would have unconsciously internalized some measure of identification with Vivian—even while she also disidentified with her—and that this would make itself felt in Karen's career choice, the one aspect of Vivian's life she could admire. Thus, not only did Karen Richards become an attorney, but she practiced the same kind of public-interest law that had engaged her adoptive mother all her life.

Was this also a daughter's way of making a last-ditch attempt to wrest some approval from this mother who treated her so harshly? Perhaps. But whatever Karen's accomplishments in the law, getting her mother's approval was not among them—a reality that was brought forcefully home when Vivian died and specifically excluded Karen from her will.

By the time she entered law school, Karen was dating Philip Richards, the man who would become her third and last husband. "He asked me to marry him, but I said, 'I don't do marriage well, but I'll live with you.'" Two years later, they did marry and have been together ever since. Soon afterward, Karen finished law school and began a successful career as a litigator in a public interest law firm.

For the first time in her life, she had everything she wanted—a man she loved, a daughter who was flourishing, and a satisfying career. True, she was working too hard, was spending too many hours at the office, was guilty about not being more available for Jennifer and Philip. But she consoled herself with the knowledge that that's what lawyers do. Then the roof fell in. While Jennifer, then about twelve, was away at camp, she took too many Excedrin tablets. It wasn't a serious suicide attempt; she took only six or seven pills. But it was a clear call for help from a child entering the bewildering maze of adolescence, a cry that was frighteningly and eerily reminiscent of Karen's own experience when, at about the same age, she took an overdose of aspirin. "It was this horrible déjà vu. The idea that *my daughter* would do that was nearly intolerable."

Karen and Philip took Jennifer to a therapist with whom she was able to examine her fears and feelings and to reestablish her equilibrium. But it was the last straw for her mother, who spiraled down into a depression from which she didn't recover for about a year. "The thing with Jennifer made me feel very vulnerable. I felt totally out of control. I could actually feel things slipping away from me, and I couldn't stop them. I was having more and more trouble making decisions. I couldn't really talk to people; it seemed like my face was paralyzed and my thinking was all fuzzy. I was losing weight, had no interest in sex, and was very guilty because Jennifer was getting short shrift from me, and I knew she needed me. But I was powerless.

"Finally, I went to see a therapist. I can remember my question to him: 'Why do I feel like I want to drive off a bridge? I have a good marriage, a good job, a good child. What's the matter with me? Can't I ever be satisfied?' He said something—asked a question, I think—and I began to cry. To my shock, when I could finally speak, I started to talk about my head being dumped in the toilet full of vomit. It was the first time I'd ever told that to anyone, and I was absolutely shocked that what was coming out of my mouth was something so ancient."

Ancient, and all but forgotten. It's not that until then she had no memory of her sufferings at Vivian Thompson's hands but that she didn't *want* to remember, that she had consciously refused to dwell on them when they arose unbidden to her mind. "I thought, what was the point? I couldn't change it. All I wanted was to get away from all that and get on with my life," she says by way of explanation.

It's just this determination to leave the past behind, her obstinate refusal to allow it to dominate the present, that enabled Karen to live a productive adulthood. Paradoxically, however, the very quality that was her strength also contained within it the seeds of her weakness because, as she found out when she succumbed to depression, the past will not be denied.

The one thing Karen never tried to forget was her Finnish family, who, although her memories were hazy at best, remained a presence in her inner life. While she lived with the fantasy that someone would one day find and reclaim her, she didn't make any serious efforts to try to find them. As a child, of course, there was nothing she could do. But even in adulthood, her efforts were sporadic and relatively undirected.

Partly this was because she didn't know where to start, since her adoptive mother refused all her requests for information about her family—who they were, where they might be, how she might contact them. And by then, Karen didn't even remember her Finnish name. But she also accepted Vivian's refusal to cooperate because she was afraid of what she might find. Would they want to see her? Was it true, as Vivian kept telling her, that they wanted nothing to do with her? That her mother was a common street whore? Moreover, at the same time that Karen yearned for this family she didn't know, she was very angry at the mother who sold her to strangers in a far-off land. So she had questions: Did she, Karen, want to know this woman?

What could her mother possibly say that would explain her behavior, that would make it understandable, if not acceptable?

As she began to emerge from her depression, however, she knew she had to act more forcefully to reclaim that part of her past. So when she heard that Vivian's cousin was coming from Finland for a family reunion, she decided to attend. "I met this woman and asked her if she could help me find my family. She looked at me kind of puzzled and said she didn't understand why I was asking, since she had given that information to Vivian about five years before. At that time, she said, my mother and my two brothers were all alive."

She interrupts her narrative and, her eyes narrowing in anger, her words acrid, says, "Of course, Vivian never told me. I found out later that my older brother, Lars, had been trying to find me for years. He even came to the United States to look for me and contacted her. She told him she didn't know where I was, which was a lie. But he didn't go away; he kept calling, so she finally told him that she'd made contact with me and that I didn't remember anyone from Finland, that I didn't want anything to do with any of them, and that I had sworn her to secrecy so she couldn't tell him where I was. She was so convincing, so sympathetic, and so sad that I was responding that way, that he believed her."

She stops speaking as she experiences again the rage she felt then. Then, shaking herself back to the present, she continues, "This cousin told me my family name, which I had completely forgotten, and she promised to make inquiries again when she got back to Finland. A couple of months later, I got a letter telling me that my mother was dead and that she was trying to reach my brothers."

Karen waited impatiently for news. But it took a few more months before her prayers were answered. As she relives the moment, she's overcome with emotion once again. "I don't think there are words to describe it," she says when she can finally speak. "It was a Sunday night, midnight, about a week before Christmas. The phone rang, and Philip picked it up, and I heard him saying, 'No, there's no one here by that name.'

"I knew immediately that this was someone from my family. I don't know how; I just knew. My heart literally leaped into my chest, and I grabbed the phone from him. I could hear the hum of the long-distance lines, then this man's deep voice came on saying his name, which I didn't understand, then saying my name—my old Finnish name—which I also didn't understand. Then, I couldn't believe it, he spoke in halting English and said, 'This is your brother Lars. I have never forgotten you, and I have loved you always.' "

Five days later, Karen was on a plane to Finland to be reunited with a family she hadn't seen for nearly forty years. "Everyone kept telling me to wait, that I didn't know anything about who they were or what I'd find. But I knew I had to go."

Today, she maintains an apartment in Finland, where she goes for a month or so each year to be received warmly and eagerly by a large family consisting of her two brothers, their children and grandchildren, and assorted aunts and uncles. When she's at home, she remains in regular mail and telephone contact with them. Her brother, Lars, spends every winter in California with Karen and her husband, where he's not just a welcome guest but a beloved member of the family with a room of his own. Another brother, Martti, and his wife have visited her there. She has a very close relationship with one of her nieces, an artist with whom she felt an immediate affinity.

But it is with Lars, the brother who never gave up hope of finding her, that she has the most intense bond—a bond, she says, that was instantaneous and that has never wavered from the moment they walked into each other's arms at the Helsinki airport. "I've never felt so comfortable with anyone. With Lars, I can just exist. I don't need to justify myself to him. I trust him not to judge me, not to pull away from me, and not to make me feel guilty if I don't do or act or produce."

For a few years after her reunion with her family, Karen's life was relatively serene. Soon after her return from her first visit to Finland, she gave up the practice of law. It was a difficult decision at the time because it meant relinquishing what had become an important part of her identity. But after recovering from her depression, she no longer was willing to give so much of herself over to it. She wanted time to watch the flowers grow; to mend her relationship with her husband, which, between her high-pressure job and her depression, had grown distant; to enjoy her brother's winter visits; to spend more time with her daughter, who was growing so quickly into womanhood.

Problems remained, of course—not least of them, if not law, what would she do with the rest of her life? With time to reflect and explore, the question began to answer itself. As she started to chronicle her daily life in her journal, she discovered that she was a potentially talented writer, and soon was directing her energies to developing that part of herself.

Whatever the uncertainties in her professional life, her family and personal life flourished. She and Philip were moving toward each other again. Jennifer had emerged from an early adolescent crisis into a warm and loving companion. Her beloved Lars was a constant in her life.

But her trials were not yet over.

On a bright spring day, about three years after Karen found her birth family, Jennifer, then nineteen years old, was about to set out on a journey with a friend. The morning was filled with the usual last-minute departure rituals. Finally, the car was packed, the farewells said, and they were off. Several hours later, Karen looked up from her dinner preparations in the kitchen to see two police officers coming up the front walk. "The doorbell rang. The dog barked. All time stopped. I just knew. I knew Jennifer was dead. I didn't want to open the door; all I could think was, 'No, please, go away; let's start this day over again.' "

How does one speak about the death of a child? It's every parent's worst nightmare, the unimaginable come true. "After my daughter's death, what is pain? It doesn't exist because nothing can ever compare with that pain," says Karen.

The months that followed that terrible day sorely tested Karen's commitment to life and sanity. For week after agonizing week, she wanted to see no one, to speak with no one. It was as if she had a No Entry sign posted on her soul. With her husband, her brother, and a few close friends standing by, she sat silently in her room, wrapped in a haze of memory and pain, communicating only with her computer as she wrote about her beloved daughter—about her inner beauty and her love of life, about her senseless death and her own despair.

Some months later, Karen Richards found her way to my office and began a course of psychotherapy that would, in some ways, affect both our lives. For me, listening to her story, watching her remarkable capacity to examine her life and herself, witnessing her resilience in the face of tragedy focused me once again on the questions I have asked for years about the sources of such transcendence—questions that ultimately led me to write this book. For her, these have been years of mourning and recovery.

Today, several years after Jennifer's death, she holds her head high once again. She has good friends and work she loves, although, like all writers, there are moments when she wonders whether the pleasure in writing, the joy in crafting that perfect sentence, is worth the pain of getting there. Her marriage is stronger than ever; her relationship with her brother, Lars, an unfailing source of comfort and pleasure. In endless talks about her early life in Finland, he fills in the blanks of her forgotten past and helps her to learn again her first language, of which she still remembers nothing. "It's amazing, isn't it?" she asks. "I was seven years old and perfectly fluent in Finnish, and I have no recollection of ever speaking it. Nothing comes back, even when I hear it."

Her connections with the surviving Thompsons are limited. Vivian and Dick are both dead. Their biological son, Ezra, who, until he ended his misery with a bullet to his brain, lived in total isolation in the family house and was incapable of sustaining any kind of human relationship. "I felt sorry for him when he was alive; he was so all alone, so I used to call once in a while," says Karen. And Benjamin, the brother she loved, is equally psychologically impaired, the barrier he built to protect himself from Vivian's anger having become nearly impenetrable. "I'm in touch with Benjamin, but it's hard to have a relationship with him because he's so cut off. It's like there's a wall that nobody can get through," she says regretfully.

Her legitimate anger at the treatment she received at Vivian Thompson's hands notwithstanding, she's able also to appreciate what was positive in that environment. "My brother, Martti, says, 'No matter how bad it was, you were still in America. Here, you would have been pregnant by the time you were sixteen, and that would have been your life.'

"Sometimes when he says things like that, it makes me angry. But," she grants, in her typical ability to see the glass as half full, "I also know that he's right. I went from the most terrible poverty to a family that had an apartment in the city and a house in the country. So I was exposed to a life I couldn't even have dreamed of in my family in Finland.

"Vivian Thompson was an educated, cultured woman. We heard good music in that house, and there were books, lots of them. I spent a lot of time listening to music and living in those books. She liked the theater, too, and since no one else in the family was interested, she'd sometimes take me with her to see a play or hear a concert. All of those are things that have given me great pleasure in my life. So even though she was so cruel and hateful to me, living there taught me things and opened up opportunities I wouldn't have had if I had stayed in Finland."

There are scars, of course. And from time to time, they bleed. Karen gives the gift of trust warily, biding her time, testing to be sure it will not be betrayed. Since no parent ever fully recovers from the loss of a child, it's not surprising that the pain of Jennifer's death still catches her up unexpectedly. She sees a healthy, bursting-with-life nineteen-year-old, and her heart weeps. Her husband's daughter has a baby, and she suffers the knowledge that Jennifer, who adored children, will never have one; that she, Karen, will never know a grandchild of her own.

With all that, however, Karen Richards looks at her life now and says, "After Jennifer died, I was afraid I'd never find joy again in the things I used to find joyful, for example, music. I wondered if that feeling would ever come back, but remarkably, it has.

"I know I'm not a Pollyannaish kind of person, and it always seems amazing to me, given my life, that I have always been able to find joy and happiness at times, even in Vivian Thompson's house. I can find it in a book, in the outdoors, in music, in lots of things, even in beating Lars at dominoes. That's delayed sibling rivalry, I suppose," she adds with a mischievous smile.

nine

Chris Lydon:
From Pimp to Professor

HE'S TALL AND SLIM, AN IMPOSING PRESENCE WITH CHOCOLATE BROWN skin, a warm smile, a strong handshake, and an African hat perched on his head. As with most of the other women and men whose stories are told in this book, we met on the telephone, introduced by a mentor from his past. Although he agreed without hesitation to my request for an interview, it took several months and as many phone conversations before he could pry the time loose from his extraordinarily busy life. Now, as he settles himself in the chair before me, my attention is caught by the restless energy he brings into the room, evident in the way he walks and talks, in the way he seems to be in motion, even when he's sitting perfectly still.

Unlike most of the others I've written about here, Chris Lydon's history doesn't feature abuse, abandonment, or even serious mistreatment—except for the kind that comes from being poor, black, and male in America. That he has known in full measure. It's precisely because race is such a central feature of his life story—because it's nearly impossible to disentangle his family experience from the social conditions of his life in an urban ghetto, because the disabling conditions of his life lie at least as much in the social world as in the familial one—that his story deserves a place on these pages.

It isn't that his life in the family was easy or that there weren't major hurdles to surmount there. His earliest recollections are of a household where there was never enough money, where people were crowded into a space too small for anyone's comfort or privacy, where there sometimes wasn't enough food on the table, where his parents' constant conflict was frightening.

But as I listen to his tale of growing up in one of Chicago's most notorious public housing projects, the family seems to have dropped out as a serious influence in his life by the time he was old enough to be out on the street alone. It's a familiar tale. In other communities, the family is the mediator between the child and the outside world, shepherding the child through his contacts with that world, protecting him from its dangers. But for the young black males who live in our urban ghettoes, the only protection they have is whatever they can create for themselves. Not usually because their families don't try to guard them from harm, but because they're helpless to do so in an environment where danger and death lurk on every corner. As Chris Lydon, himself now a father, says bitterly, "In the African American community, you're afraid to hear the phone ring after a certain time of night because you just know it's going to be that somebody's dead or in big trouble. And as a parent, hard as you try, there's nothing you can do to prevent it."

It's not just the mean streets that make life so difficult for the young boys who live on them. It's also the pain and anger that go with being black and male in this society—the sense of futility that comes from knowing you're a despised and unwelcome intruder in your own land; the conviction that the future holds no more promise than the present; the anguish and rage that come from being a permanent suspect, from knowing that you instill fear in the hearts of your countrymen simply by your presence on the street.

Like so many young black men have done before and since, Chris reacted to these realities with behavior that nearly destroyed his life. Now, as I listen to the story of his past and try to fit it into what I know of his present, I find myself thinking, *It's not what he did then but what he is now that's so surprising. What enabled him to see an exit when others around him could not?* For this man, who, at fifty, holds a doctorate in psychology, was a thief at twelve, in a juvenile facility at sixteen, a pimp at twenty, and a con man at twenty-two, and somewhere along the way, fathered six children who were born of four different mothers.

Now in his packed professional life, he's a staff psychologist in a social agency, teaches in a graduate training program, and is a consultant to several community organizations dedicated to helping families and children survive the rigors of inner-city life. All this while he juggles a rising career as an actor and is raising his two youngest children, ages six and ten, alone.

His man-in-a-hurry expression relaxes a bit when I ask him to talk about his early childhood, and his body tension eases as he thinks back to the past. "In my family, there were five kids, my mama and daddy, and my uncle and his wife and their two children. Other people moved in, too, when they needed help. My uncles, when they came back from the Korean War, stayed with us. So it was real crowded; there were only three bedrooms for all those people. And there was no privacy because the walls were so thin you could hear everything that was going on in the other apartments.

"It had its good points, though," he adds quickly, not wanting to sound as if he's complaining. "In those days, the kids would go back and forth to each other's apartments all the time. The one thing you could never do was eat there, though, even if people offered you food," he says with a grimace as he recalls the rumblings in his empty stomach. "Sometimes I'd be smelling the food and starving, but I'd never say, yes, I want it. That was absolutely discouraged by all the parents. I guess they didn't want you to take food from people when maybe they didn't have enough for themselves."

But it wasn't simply that these parents didn't want their children taking food from people who needed it. It was also their pride—the pride of the poor who need to present a self-respecting face to the world; the pride of parents who, already suffering the private humiliation of knowing that their children often leave the table hungry, try to protect themselves from the public shame as well. If their children are taught to refuse food when it's offered, they can live with the illusion that no one will ever know they can't always provide it.

"I still see it right now in certain southern families," continues Chris. "The kids come in, and you ask if they want something to eat, and they say no. I can tell they do, but their parents warned them never to act like they're hungry. I guess they don't want anybody to think they sent their kids out hungry."

Chris's father, James Lydon, did "little odds-and-ends jobs if he worked at all"—a fate that's common to many men in inner-city black families, where the women are able to find some kind of menial work and the men either are unemployed or make do with odd jobs when they're available. Marguerite Lydon, Chris's mother, was a food-service worker in a local hospital, an exhausting job that paid poorly, but that had one advantage: She could save money by bringing leftovers home.

At first, Chris is reluctant to talk about his parents' relationship with each other or his relationship with them. It's the kind of loyalty I see often in adult children of poor and working-class families, loyalty born of the understanding that their parents' lives were so difficult, their options so limited. "There's not a lot to talk about," he says hesitantly. "It was an ordinary, traditional African American family. We were poor, but it wasn't their fault. It's just what life was like in the African American community." He pauses, trying to decide whether to speak his thoughts, then continues, "I feel kind of funny saying things about them; I wouldn't want to hurt their feelings. They did the best they could."

But as his guard drops, he begins to talk more openly about the conflict between his mother and father. "They argued a lot, and it upset me," he recalls. "My mama, she's pretty feisty, a lot more than my daddy, and she has a real sharp mouth. It used to get pretty wild, and sometimes I was afraid he'd hit her. I don't think he ever did, but I remember once seeing her hit him with a shoe. I also remember one time they were having this big argument, and he kept trying to get at her, and I was holding him back. He kept hollering to let him go, and my mama kept saying to hang on. I hated those arguments; I wanted to jump out the window and run," he concludes, a fleeting look of distaste crossing his mobile features.

Despite the crowded living conditions, Chris Lydon was a lonely child who often hungered for something he still can't easily define. He talks a great deal about food—about the leftovers his mother brought from the hospital that he didn't like, about the breakfasts his father cooked that displeased him. "It seemed like either I didn't have enough to eat or it wasn't the right kind of food." But as I listen to him return time and again to the subject of eating, it's hard to think that it was just food he was missing. Rather, his talk of food seems to reflect his feeling that he never got all he wanted and needed, a sense of deprivation partly because, he says, "I wasn't really *in* the family."

Asked what this means, he looks puzzled as he tries to find the words, then replies thoughtfully, "It's kind of hard to say exactly. It isn't that they didn't treat me right. But in the African American community they want their boys to grow up to be *big men*," he says, emphasizing the words and raising his widespread arms high above his head to demonstrate how big they're expected to be, "so they treat them a lot rougher than they treat a girl. When you're a kid, that doesn't feel good."

He pauses to reflect on his words, then explains, "The initial intentions are good, to teach the boys how to take care of themselves. I used to do it with my younger brothers, make them fight each other, because I thought it would make them tough. My kids do it with my grandkids now. Everybody needs to know that, I guess, and if you're black and male you *really* need to. But it's not a good start for a kid, especially in these times. With all the violence the kids are living in, it seems to me they're only gearing the kids up for more of that kind of violence," he concludes, his voice rising in anger.

He stirs restlessly, gets up and walks around the room, and says, "Maybe I never felt like I was really *in* anyplace, and I wanted to be. I always wanted to do something with my life, something different; I just didn't know how then—and nobody around me did, either."

For a poor black boy in Chicago's ghetto, a child in a family where daily life was a struggle for survival, the possibilities for "something different" were few and the choices nearly nonexistent. Choice not only requires knowledge of the alternatives and how to find them, it means believing that they're possible. But Chris, whose parents were unable to envision a future much different from the present— whether for themselves or for their children—knew little about the possibilities and even less about how to reach for them.

It wasn't only the disadvantage of poverty that limited his choices and dampened his spirit. He also grew up in a world that consistently devalued him because he was black. He lived in a segregated community where resources, whether public or private, were few; where crime and drugs were part of life's daily ration; where schools often were little more than holding cells that passed students through even when they couldn't read. "I did badly in school," muses Chris. "It wasn't the kind of place to make you want to do well. And nobody cared. In high school I used to sleep and slobber on my math book and I passed. When I graduated, I didn't have the basic skills you need to get along. It was a terrible struggle later when I was in college and graduate school and had to take statistics courses. I had no background at all for it."

The near-total isolation of the community Chris lived in made it difficult, if not impossible, to know what the "something different" he yearned for might be. At the same time, his conviction that he was unwelcome in the larger world made it virtually impossible for him to try to find his way into it. "People don't like poor folk anyway. Then if you're black and poor, they like you even less. And if you're black and poor and male and young, nobody's got any use for you at all."

For Chris Lydon, America is, indeed, what sociologist Andrew Hacker has called "two nations," its racial divide burned deep in his soul. "It's unfortunate that race is an issue, but it is," he says with conviction. "People respond to people's color and class in socially learned, tainted ways; even black people do. I teach my kids never to call anybody out because of their race, and I feel good because they don't do things like that. But it's not the way with most folks, black or white.

"When I was growing up, black people talked like they hated whites because of what they did to them, but then they believed the things they said. In my family I'd always hear how white folks do terrible things and how they're racist. But at the same time, I remember how black was a bad color; your hair was bad; your skin color was bad. The white man was the smart guy. If a black man and a white man said different things, you listened to the white guy because he knew better," he recalls, his expression caught between understanding and contempt.

It's precisely this disorienting contest between thought and feeling—the anger at white stereotypes while also internalizing them—that is one of the most tragic consequences of racism. "It's like you believed two opposite things at the same time, which could make a person crazy," Chris concludes sadly.

Until now, a central argument in this book has been that a sense of marginality in the family, the child's feeling that he doesn't fit, lays the psychological groundwork that enables the growing child to see and grasp alternatives. For Chris, the script reads somewhat differently. It's true that, in the long run, his sense of marginality, of not really belonging anywhere—in the family or on the street—eventually led him to reach for positive alternatives when they were finally

put before him. In the short run, however, given who he was and
where he lived, the only option he saw didn't save his life, it nearly
destroyed it.

It was the promise of the street, the comradeship and sense of
belonging that's forged among the "boys in the 'hood," that com-
bined with his distance and alienation from the larger white world to
determine the path he took. It was in that larger world, the world
where he still bears the mark of stigma because he's black, that he felt
his marginality most keenly. His deep-seated sense of otherness, his
understanding that he was scorned by the white world, that his blackness was reviled, that he could never belong, made it easy to turn to
the street—a turn that was facilitated by an alienated community
whose youths had nowhere of consequence to go.

When Chris was twelve, John D, a boy who would become his best
friend through most of his teenage years, moved into the projects.
The two quickly became inseparable. "John D and me," he says, his
face crinkling into a loving smile, "we had a relationship everybody
in the community knew about, even the police." He stops speaking
and stares out the window for a few moments. When he resumes, his
words are etched in sorrow, "John D was killed by the police during
one of those riots back then. He was about twenty. A lot of the guys I
hung with then are dead or in the joint."

After John D came into his life, Chris didn't feel alone anymore.
For the first time he had a soul mate, someone who understood what
he thought and felt, whose unquestioning acceptance comforted
him and eased his loneliness. As I listen to his description of this
friendship, I'm struck with how much he sounds like a person who
has fallen in love. "I always had this feeling of being alone until I met
John D. I think I kind of had this pitiful look, at least that's the way I
felt. After we got to be friends, I felt more at home in myself. I can't
really explain it. It was like I had somebody. We had a life and could
have fun. Those were real good times."

Part of the "fun" and the "good times" was learning how to become a thief. "When John D and I got together is when we started stealing. We'd go downtown during the holidays and steal everybody's presents. Not just for them, we stole for ourselves, too," he says with a laugh.

"After awhile people would send us down to steal—other kids in the neighborhood, John D's older brother, people like that. They'd tell us what they wanted, and we'd go get it. We'd do that every Saturday; then on Sunday we'd go down and sneak into the show. We'd sneak out in the middle and go to the big drugstore on the corner, steal a bunch of candy or whatever else we wanted, then go back in and see the rest of the show."

"Did our parents know?" he asks, echoing my question. "They had to have known. Where else would we be getting all that stuff from? But nobody ever said anything. Sometimes, when I'd come in with a bunch of stuff, my mama would say, 'You better not have stolen it.' But she didn't really mean it. She thought the white man was getting what he deserved if we took his goods. My daddy, he cared. But mama pretty much ruled the roost."

I'm caught, as I listen to his words, one side of me dismayed by a parent who closes her eyes to this kind of antisocial behavior, the other side remembering my own mother who didn't set a sterling example of rectitude for her children either. In all my years as a child in New York, for example, she never paid my way onto the subway, pushing me under the turnstile instead, even when I was already half grown. There were times, too, when the family fell out of the working poor and was forced onto welfare. Like so many women in that position, she often found some kind of work to supplement the inadequate dole and coached my brother and me with the lies we were to tell the welfare worker when she came around with her questions. My mother also worked insurance scams, threatening suit for some injury, usually contrived—a nuisance threat the insurance companies often settled for some paltry sum that looked big to my mother's impoverished eyes.

I haven't thought about these things for many years, probably because they filled me with shame when I was a child. But I wonder as I write these words now if this isn't one of the social costs of poverty and alienation. For it's hard for people who feel abused and victimized by society to believe in its rules. In my mother's case, it wasn't just survival that motivated her behavior, there was also an element of retribution. When the company that held my father's tiny life insurance policy went bankrupt and refused to pay her claim after his death, she was left with a deep-seated sense of injury, a conviction that the system had failed her and that, therefore, she was entitled to wrest from it what she could.

I don't know if it's that kind of experience, and the sensibility that can flow from it, that silenced Marguerite Lydon. I do know, however, that talking about his career as a thief evokes neither shame nor guilt for her son, who says, "What do you expect? You don't give a kid a fair break, why should he care?" And I also know that what finally stopped his stealing was not some inner conviction that it was wrong. Instead, he continued to shoplift well into adulthood, stopping only after he finally gained a stake in the system.

As a professional man, Chris had a reason to care, a reputation to protect, a way of life at risk. "I didn't have any guilt about stealing from a store then, and I still wouldn't, except that my religion now tells me I shouldn't," he says. "That makes a difference, but I think mostly what stops me now is I wouldn't want to get caught. Before, I had nothing to lose, so I didn't give a damn about getting caught. But now my reputation and my place in the community are important, and with that comes a lot more responsibility. So I think about how embarrassing it would be if I got caught."

Now, however, as he speaks about his career as a thief, he tells his story easily, taking pleasure in his ability to do it well. "I used to love it—the thrill of it, getting the stuff. I was real good at it, too; I rarely ever got caught."

The satisfaction that colors his words isn't simply a response to the status and approval his daring and competence brought him on the street. That was important, to be sure. But equally important was his pride in doing something well, a quality that has served him throughout his life, whether in thievery in his youth or in overcoming the deficits of his failed earlier education to get through college and a doctoral program in adulthood. He brought the same energy, the same intelligence, the same street smarts, to both enterprises. For whenever he decided that the game was worth the candle—whether in the criminal world or in the straight one—his performance was beyond criticism.

When Chris was sixteen, he and two friends were picked up for involvement in some illegal gang activities. "The other guys were caught red-handed," he says, "but it wasn't so clear with me, so I probably didn't have to go to jail. But my friend, Jerome—he died of a heroin overdose a few years later—was afraid he couldn't make it without me in there with him. So when we came before the judge, I said whatever I needed to say to go to jail with him."

I listen with astonishment, wondering what would possibly make a sixteen-year-old practically volunteer to go to a juvenile detention facility. I know that the bonds between these youths can be extraordinarily powerful, partly perhaps because their lives are at such risk, because there are so few places where they feel safe and protected, so few where they can belong, where they feel validated and affirmed. I know, too, that they live by a moral code that requires them to stand by each other in a kind of loyalty that transcends almost any other consideration. But going to jail? "I guess it's hard to explain," Chris says with a laugh. "You see, we were good friends, hugging friends, and we did for each other. I knew he'd have trouble there without me. The fact is, he found it real hard and kept wanting us to run away. But I'd talk him out of it."

The importance of being "hugging friends" notwithstanding, Chris's words also suggest that, even if not at a wholly conscious level, he was glad to be taken off the street. "I was in the gang because it was cool," he observes. "We couldn't wait until Friday night when we'd all put on our beautiful red gang jackets, get some cheap wine, and go out and look for somebody to fight. But, you know, I guess I sort of knew I didn't want to keep doing what I was doing, running the streets like that. You keep doing it because it's what they want to do, and they're your friends, and," he hesitates, searches for words, then says with a shrug, "it's your life, that's all; it's what there is."

He stops again, reflects on what he's just said, and backtracks, "Well, I guess it's not *all* there is, is it? In some ways I was always out of place, whether I was on the street or in college. Even when I was in my teens and doing all that stuff, I wanted to do something with my life, to make something of it. But nobody else wanted to do what I wanted to do, and until they got married or went away, I couldn't do anything else either. It was like I just needed to be with them."

It seems, then, that whatever the problems of being locked up, there was also some relief for Chris—the relief of an enforced respite from the streets, of having the opportunity to think about what he was doing with his life. At the same time, he hated being confined. In characteristic fashion, however, instead of indulging in fantasies about running away, as his friend did, he became a leader, a model prisoner who was soon chosen to be the inmate mayor of the institution. "I made up my mind that I wasn't going to be there one minute more than I had to, and I was going to do what I had to do to make sure I got out as soon as possible."

A year or so later he was released and went back to finish high school. At first, he says, he was up to the same old tricks, cutting school, paying no attention when he was there. But like the others I've written about in this book, Chris has always had that quality of adoptability, that capacity not only to attract people who were willing to teach and support him but to use what they offered. "There was always someone who would hold out a hand at the right moment. It didn't have anything to do with what they'd get back, and there was nothing gimmicky or self-aggrandizing or self-centered about it.

They were just good folk who wanted to see me get out of the rain, do well in the class, or just feel good about myself. Even when I was in grammar school, there would be one interesting teacher, some nice woman who cared and got me interested in something she was teaching."

This time around, the "nice woman" who led him "out of the rain" succeeded in interesting him in reading. For those of us who have always been at ease with books, it's hard to imagine what it's like suddenly to discover the pleasure of reading. For Chris Lydon, it was a profoundly important life-shaping event. For the first time ever, he had something other than his friends on the street to keep him company. He could lose himself in a book.

From then on, he lived a dual life, part of him deeply immersed in the street culture, the other part trying to fulfill his desire to "do something" with his life. He thought about going to college, but, he says, "I never really believed I could do it. After I graduated from high school, I went up to the local community college one day, but when I looked in the door and didn't see anybody who looked like me, I turned around and left. It took four more years before I ever went back."

When, in the mid-1960s, the Manpower Training Program, an agency of Lyndon Johnson's War on Poverty, opened an office in his neighborhood, he was first in line. "I saw it as a chance," he says. There, he met Linda Martin, a black psychologist who became, in his words, "the most critical influence in my life. She was older and wiser, and she gave me a lot. She was pretty; she was nice; she liked me; she didn't patronize me; and she wanted me to do well," he says, ticking off her qualities as if from a list imprinted on his brain. "From the time I met her, I knew that I wanted to be a psychologist and work with her."

But his involvement with Linda and the program didn't affect his activities on the street, where he was running gambling games, pimping, playing the con, and occasionally dealing drugs. "I was talking with Linda a lot about what I could be doing with my life, and I was also out hustling on the street. I never sold heroin, though," he says, as if to establish the limits of what he was willing to do. "When I sold drugs, it was cocaine; that was the fashionable in-crowd drug. But selling cocaine wasn't a status thing to pimps. You were just a dope dealer. So I stopped doing that because I wanted to have the status of pimps and con folk.

"The con game's the most respectable on the street. You make more money with less toll on folks. But you also get more time for it because Americans don't like it if you violate the one thing that's sacred to them—money. If you shoot and kill, you get five or six months. Take their money, and it's twenty years," he concludes in a cynical and contemptuous evaluation of our justice system and the values it embodies.

Unfortunately, the Manpower Training Program was starved for funds and soon foundered. "Something happened, and it just disappeared. One day it just wasn't there anymore," he says, the bewilderment he felt then still apparent now.

With the program's demise, his budding relationship with Linda Martin was aborted as well—a loss that left him distressed and lonely but determined to walk through the door of the community college that had seemed so daunting a few years earlier. "That was a time," he says, shaking his head at the memory. "I snorted coke, drank whiskey, ran the streets until five in the morning, slept until seven-thirty, got up and drove to school in my black Cadillac. I was twenty-two."

At college, he discovered drama and began to take classes because, he says airily but not wholly convincingly, "The con is an act, and I figured if I learned to act, I could do it better." It's certainly true that, whatever other qualities are evident in street life, it is also theater—the roles, the props, the costumes, the posturing. Chris's swagger, the way he dressed, the car he drove, the woman on his arm—all these were part of the role he assumed the moment he stepped onto the street, which was his stage.

But it wasn't just the wish to perfect his street act that drew Chris to study acting. He also understood, even if only intuitively, that his acting could become a rehearsal for another life. Long before he stepped into that classroom, he knew from his experience on the street that an actor doesn't just *act* a part, he *becomes* it, at least while on stage. For Chris, whose main "act" until then was the hip, fast-talking, street-smart con artist, studying acting was a legitimate way of trying on other roles, of experiencing other ways of being, even if only briefly. In doing so, he could find parts of himself that were otherwise unavailable, parts that could take him to the different life he wanted.

And, in fact, acting has been an important element in his growth and development, eventually taking the place of his activities on the street. The theater offered some of the same challenge, the same excitement, the same sense of adventure, the same fun that he found in the con, while it also opened up the possibilities for personal change he hadn't known before. "I liked drama; I liked being backstage. I'd read a play, and it would come alive in my head. It was exciting.

"Later on I met this director who had this little theater where he used to do a lot of black plays. He's another one who gave me something very, very important and taught me a lot. I was slowly coming off the street at the time and had no training. But he encouraged me. I stayed involved with him and the theater for years. I didn't know anything about getting paid for acting then; it was just fun. I hung around there a lot, sometimes sixteen hours a day, so I didn't have much time for getting into trouble."

At the time he took his first acting class, however, all that was still in the future. Then, he was still deeply engaged in his chaotic life on the street, while also doing well enough at the two-year community college he was attending to think about transferring to the university. It wasn't until the Black Panthers arrived in the community, offering support, encouragement, and a job program, that he was able to turn the dream into a reality. "The Panthers were a real inspiration to me.

They wanted to help kids like me do something else with our lives. I got a job in their summer youth program, and they kept encouraging me and telling me I should go to the university, that I could do it if I wanted to. They said, 'You go, we'll get you some money.' So I applied and got in."

At the university he met Linda Martin again and, soon afterward, joined a psychotherapy group she headed. "I was still driving the Cadillac and playing both sides of the street, and I told them all about what I was doing. I had rationalized everything and was feeling pretty good about it. It was like, this is what you have to do to get along."

The men he met in the group were awed by his exploits, urging him on with their admiration and esteem. "They'd listen to me talk and say, 'Great man! Wow! Good deal!'" recalls Chris. But not the women. They offered criticism not praise, contempt not honor. "The women helped me. They didn't think what I was doing on the street was such a good deal; they were real upset about it. And after awhile, they made me feel it wasn't such a good idea, too. So slowly I stopped doing it."

"Why would the women's disapproval have been so important?" I wonder aloud. "Don't you know the only reason men ever do anything is to impress women?" he quips laughingly. Perhaps. But this is also a good example of the power of a reference group in framing our lives. Until he entered this therapy group, the friends to whom he was so deeply attached were, like the men in the group, admiring of his successes and egging him on to greater feats of daring. They were his reference group, the people he wanted to impress, whose admiration and acceptance he sought. Now, for the first time in his life, there was a group of people who counted, whose good opinion mattered to him, who were scornful of the life he had chosen. As he met success in the straight world and his identification began to shift from con artist to college man, they became the reference group against which to judge and measure his behavior.

During this time, he and Linda became lovers. "It was a love affair that lasted about twenty years, even when I didn't see her," he says, his expression suggesting that it is perhaps still not over. "We met in 1964 when I started the Manpower Training Program, and I saw her almost daily, although we weren't involved sexually then. That came later, when I met her the second time, and lasted about ten or twelve years. There's no measuring her influence in my life. I wanted to do all this for her. If it weren't for her, I'd be dead or in the penitentiary."

True, perhaps, but equally important in keeping him alive was his ability to appreciate what Linda Martin and others put before him. One of the qualities that's so striking about Chris—a quality he shares with other transcenders—is his gratitude for small favors, the ability to see kindness in a gesture that others might take for granted. "Sometimes it's the little things other people do—the small gestures that are framed in kindness—that make a difference; sometimes it's just who they are," he says as he talks about Ken McGuire, an African American psychologist who befriended him when he first became a student. "With Ken McGuire it was both. He was the first black male college professor I ever knew, so just knowing him was something. He was always ready to help me and teach me what I needed to know. And once he actually even came to my house and took me bowling, too. I'll never forget that time," he says, the tone of his voice still reflecting the wonder of the event.

Once Chris's feet were on the path, he never got off. Although he lacked the basic skills needed to get through college, he wouldn't give up. "I struggled real hard, especially with the writing skills. But they didn't just pass me like they did in high school. I had two teachers at the university—a man and a woman, both white—who I felt I could really trust. They helped me through, but they also made me work and learn. I remember once I sat up all night writing a paper, and then Gwen, my professor, said it was so bad that I had to take it home and do it all over again. Boy, that was something, but I did it until she liked it."

It wasn't until he began to believe that he actually might earn a college degree that he severed his last ties with his life on the street. "I didn't cut everything loose until I was real close to getting a B.A. Until then, I was scared to say I can do this and drop everything else, so I had one leg on this side of the track and one on the other side. It felt safer that way."

In a symbolic gesture to signify his new life, he gave up the Cadillac and bought a Volkswagen. But it took more than symbolism to keep him safe from the lure of the streets. "I was afraid if I stayed in the neighborhood, it would jeopardize things because I'd lose my concentration there." So he moved to the dorms at school, where he remained for the next few years.

By then he was the father of four children born of three different mothers. Unlike the stereotype of the absent African American father, Chris has always been deeply involved in the lives of his children, not just as a provider but as a caretaker. Two of the children, a son, Mario, and a daughter, Shawna, were in his custody during these years because their mother had gone to New York to try to make her way as an actress. Another son, Raymond, lived with his mother, who had moved to another city. Only his son, Nathan, was not yet actively in his life because Chris didn't find out he was the boy's father until Nathan was sixteen years old.

Since he couldn't take Mario and Shawna with him into the dorms, his mother took over their daily care. He worried about leaving them, fearing that they would feel abandoned, but he saw no choice. He knew he was at risk of being pulled back into the old life if he stayed in the neighborhood. "It's hard to keep clean if you're around a lot of dirt," he says.

"I felt bad about leaving the kids like that," he explains, his expression reflecting the sadness he still feels when he thinks about it now. "My mother took good care of them, but they wanted me to be there. I spent a lot of time with them, even though I wasn't living with them, but it wasn't enough. I know they're still angry about that. They see me now with the younger kids, and they feel bad that they didn't get what I give them. I feel real bad that it wasn't enough, but I didn't know what else I could do," he says regretfully. "I don't know if you ever get it right as a parent," he concludes with a sigh, "but if I could do anything over, it would be to parent my kids again."

His remorse notwithstanding, living in the dorms was an enormous relief from the dangers and distractions of life in the neighborhood. It was as if he couldn't allow himself to know fully the hazards of his earlier life—how wearing it was to live always looking over his shoulder, how much energy it took to stay ahead of the game—until he moved into a setting that didn't require his constant vigilance. "I couldn't believe it; I had a ball in the dorm because life was so easy there. You were safe; you didn't have to watch your back; and everybody was studying. I never lived like that before."

The thrill of finishing college was matched only by his acceptance to a master's program in psychology. Although he had by then made up some of the deficiencies of his earlier education, graduate work required both a set of skills and a level of self-confidence he still didn't have. "It looked like the other students were pretty sure they knew what they were doing, but a lot of the time I felt like I was groping around, trying to stay alive. The clinical work was okay, but I struggled real hard with the writing; that was still a real big problem."

But he never considered giving it up. It was this kind of determination, his refusal to walk away even in his darkest moments, that not only saw him through but that attracted the attention of the man who would become his mentor. "There was this professor who was my adviser, he hung in there with me all the way. I still don't really like the thesis I wrote, but the two of us went over and over and over it until both of us felt okay about it. I don't know if I could have done it without him."

No sooner did he finish his master's program, than Linda Martin began to encourage him to go for a doctorate. But getting a Ph.D. was nearly incomprehensible to Chris. It wasn't the work involved that seemed so impossible, it was the very idea. *Chris Lydon, the con man, a doctor?* It was incongruous, as if this whole life must certainly be happening to another person. And in some way it was. For the man who was considering whether to apply to a Ph.D. program was not the same one who had entered that junior college classroom so tentatively so many years earlier.

The whole process of getting from there to here—the experiences he had along the way, the people he met, the parts of himself he uncovered—had changed him irreparably. It isn't that the old Chris was wholly gone. In fact, the same qualities that made him successful on the street—the energy, the intelligence, the determination, the refusal to see himself as a victim, to resign himself helplessly to the fate of his parents and peers—were also responsible for his success in his new life. But the con artist had become an actor, and the street-smart kid had become a scholar—testimony to the kind of developmental change that's possible when the social conditions are right.

After a year of struggling with himself, he applied and was accepted to a doctoral program. There he met George Morgan, a black professor who took him under his wing. "He told me I should never mistake a lack of skills for a lack of intelligence, and he made me see that writing is not intelligence; it's a skill," he recalls. "Just like you learn how to read and how to dance, you learn how to write. That helped me put it in perspective."

But there were other issues that got in his way. The sense of isolation, the knowledge that he was so different from those around him, the distance he was traveling from his former life, the fear that his success in this endeavor risked some essential core of self—all these made his passage difficult and troubling. In addition, there were the racial insults, overt and covert, to which he was subjected regularly. "At one point I was ready to beat up this teacher who I still think was a racist. But George said, 'Don't do anything; let me handle it. Then, instead of them saying there's a crazy nigger acting the fool, they'll have to say there's a crazy nigger with a Ph.D. acting the fool.'"

He pauses a moment and laughs as he savors the incident in the retelling, then says, "It wasn't funny then. In that kind of environment, you get to think there's something wrong with you because you're different. I used to leave the school and go back to the projects just to see people who were like me so I could feel like myself again. I needed to do that to remind myself that I was okay. That may be the hardest thing, not having anybody around who looks like you so you feel so different all the time. It crunches up your soul."

It was during this period that Chris turned to religion, not to the black church in which he had been raised, but to an African one—Yoruba. "I wish I'd been involved in this religion much earlier. It would have made a big difference in my life. It has made me cognizant of what's rewarded and what's repaid. Kindness is rewarded; wickedness is repaid. I take that very seriously and work on myself not to do wicked things.

"When I got involved with it, I also saw how the Yoruba religion relates to the theater. In Yoruba there's the *odu*, the one who reads and acts out the parables. That's what I want to be, the *odu*. So since I got into this religion, the theater has become even more important to me. But it's not just doing theater in this company and in this play. I want to see how to make it a part of my life and how to use it in my religion."

Today, Chris is a devoutly religious man, actively involved in both Yoruba and the theater, although he hasn't yet become an *odu*. He has, however, been a serious drama student for some years now, a commitment that has won him important roles in local theater productions. "I've learned so much more than I ever knew about how to read plays and act in them. It's been an inspiration. What I want to do now is write a play. I still don't do the writing thing well, but I'd like to try it some day."

Professionally, his life is overfull, at least partly because he's taken it as his mission to bring hope to young people who have all but lost it. It's work that keeps him connected to the African American community, work that enables him to pay back some of what he calls the "good fortune" that allowed him to get out. When he wins one, the satisfaction is enormous. But too often he finds himself frustrated and depressed by the tidal wave of violence and misery that has engulfed our inner-city black communities.

In his personal life, there are gaps. He now has two more children, ages six and ten, the products of a relationship that ended when their mother turned to crack. So he raises them alone and complains, "It's murdering me raising these two kids by myself and not having anyone to smile with. There's no one to say, 'Why don't you take them now?' 'Why don't you talk to me about this?' 'Let's do this together.' It's all yours. Single parenting should be a crime.

"I've done just about all I can do myself. I need a partner, someone I really like, who turns me on, and who's comfortable with my kids. They need to see me with somebody and know it's possible to be intimate with another person. It's important for them to see that two people can have a fight and work it out."

The words are heartfelt, the feelings that underlie them clearly evident in the room. But until now, he has been unable to make that level of commitment to a woman. "I always thought if I got married, maybe I'd see somebody else that looked better."

It isn't just his fear that somebody else would "look better," however. His inability to commit also is born, at least in part, of his sense that he has never fully belonged anywhere, that no matter what he was doing or who he was with, a part of him has always remained watchful. "It's like I've always been an observer even when it looks like I'm right in there," he says wistfully.

In his earlier years, being the observer was a functional adaptation, since it allowed him to maintain a safe distance from people and events that could have been hurtful. But once entrenched, such psychological mechanisms don't just fall away simply because they're no longer necessary. For Chris, therefore, what was adaptable then is costly now, especially in the realm of intimate relationships. He can't both stand outside and watch and also be a fully engaged participant. And the kind of partnership he now says he wants requires a level of intimate engagement that, except with his children, he has avoided for the whole of his adult life.

While trying to give his younger children the care they need poses one set of problems, keeping the lives of his older ones on track is another. As I listen to him speak repeatedly about his fears for their future, I can't help wondering: *What was he thinking about when he had all those children? How did he think he could keep them safe?* I ask the questions; his answers are murky and insubstantial. "It wasn't like I was thinking at all. And I wasn't going out trying to get folks pregnant. I was irresponsible, and they were, too. Or maybe not; maybe they wanted to have babies. With the first one, Mario, I was surprised when she got pregnant, but I wanted a baby. All my friends had babies."

Now those babies have grown, and they're a constant source of worry to their father who watches helplessly as they falter. Only Nathan, the son he didn't meet until he was sixteen, graduated from college. Mario got through high school, but the other two, Raymond and Shawna, dropped out. Although none of the four is presently married, three of them have five children between them. Raymond has had several brushes with the law and has spent some time in prison. "He's always lived on the edge and is still hanging around on the street looking for trouble," Chris says worriedly. Shawna is a welfare mother who, according to her father, "lies a lot, doesn't work, has no skills, and can't handle her money."

Reflecting on the particular difficulties facing his African American sons, Chris leans forward, his shoulders hunched, his hands spread wide in a gesture of helplessness, and says, "I've got four sons, and if I keep one of those boys out of trouble, I'll be lucky. But what can you do? Even if you drag these kids home, what are you going to do then? Handcuff them to you?"

His living arrangements, too, leave him wanting for more. He lives once again in his old neighborhood and grumbles, "I'm afraid to let my kids out the door. It's a war zone. I live with a shotgun beside my door and keep my kids inside. They ask to go play in the yard, and I say, 'No, there's poison out there.' If I agree and let them go outside, I can't rest because I'm always looking out to see if they're okay."

He turns inward, his eyes remote, his usually mobile face still. After a few silent moments, he pulls himself back into the room and continues with a sigh. "I don't know how anybody gets out; I don't even know for sure how I did. I'm the only one in the family. I've got one brother who's unemployed, another one who died of a heroin overdose, and a sister who deals drugs."

He's angry about what has happened to the old neighborhood. "When I was coming up, there was some kind of a community; now it's all gone. You didn't have to worry about kids going out and getting killed on the street then. We had our gangs, and we'd fight, and we did lots of bad things, but there were no guns."

He abhors the drugs, violence, and disorganization that's epidemic now. "In the short blessing that God gives you, I've seen quite a bit. I've been both an underachiever and an overachiever, which gives me a pretty broad lens to look out on life. But what I see now is criminal.

"I told people fifteen years ago that crack was a killer, but nobody paid attention because they were all making money out of crack, even the treatment programs," he says bitterly. "I deserve a little bit more tranquility than you can get living here."

Yet he stays. Asked why, he has a list of reasons. His older children live there, and he still holds the hope that his presence close by will help avert a disaster. His parents, too, still live in the projects, and being close to his mother makes it easy for her to answer his occasional calls for help with the younger children. Although the little ones live with him, they're attached to their own mother, so he hesitates to move them away. "She's a crack addict and not doing real good," he observes sadly, "but she's still their mama, the only one they're ever going to get."

There's undoubtedly truth in the reasons he gives. But there's also something more that keeps him in a neighborhood where he asks, "How can you cleanse your soul if you're around all that wickedness?" That "something more" is connected to race.

Chris Lydon, like most black professionals, spends his days in a dominantly white world. To make his way there, he has to walk, talk, dress in the socially prescribed style. He must, in essence, become white—or at least behave as if he is. It's only then, if at all, that the world he works in, the world where most of his waking hours are spent, "forgives" his blackness.

With few colleagues who look like him, who understand the strain of, in his words, "feeling like they're always looking and waiting," going back into the community he called home for so long is reassuring, even when it's also a difficult and dangerous place to live. It's comfortably familiar there, a place where he knows who he is and can see others like himself; where he can take off the mask, loosen the tie, and unbutton the collar; where the less constrained, street-smart style that's so much a part of him can breathe naturally once again.

It's there, too, that he can remain connected to his past, to the people who knew him in his earlier life, to the friends he once loved. "How do you know who you are if you just forget the past?" he asks. "There's a lot in your old life that's important, and old friends are *real* important. When I hear someone call out *Bro*—that's what they used to call me when I was a kid—it feels real good, and I pay attention because I know they're from my past."

He stops speaking for a few moments, then, his voice filled with longing, says, "I wish some of those old friends were here now and could be with me in the work I'm doing. We'd be the baddest group of psychologists anywhere. But the only way those guys stayed together is when they went to jail. It's the same thing now with my sons and their friends. If you go into the pen and find a gang, you'll find out they were friends since they were thirteen."

Whatever the comfort in staying in the old neighborhood, it's also a costly choice, as Chris knows all too well. "There's hardly a family in the African American community that's not living in fear; they're just sitting and waiting for trouble. The Ku Klux Klan doesn't have to shoot anybody anymore; they're killing themselves. You've got these three-strike laws and a bunch of new prisons, but these kids just don't care. Everybody else lives in fear, but they *expect* to die.

"A lot of black kids don't like that stuff. But they can't do anything about it. There's no protection. Parents used to be able to protect their kids, but they can't do that anymore. So the kids just give up. When I work with them, I try to pull for the part of them that wants to survive. But even when you've got a good family situation to work with, it's real hard for the kids to see a way out, no matter what you tell them. Then, when they've got a mama on crack and they've seen the worst things you can imagine, it's nearly impossible to make them care.

"I love my kids and I love African American people, but I don't like what's happening. The shooting and killing are unforgivable. The lack of compassion they have for each other, or for anyone else, is terrible. I can't support that; I won't," he says, his words angry, his expression anguished.

He looks away, visibly agitated as he contemplates what has happened to the black community. "I've been able to live my life from a nearly empty glass to an almost full one. You can't ask more than that, can you? It was good fortune that made the difference, and meeting good people who helped me do the right thing and become what I am. Today," he says, his head bowed in despair, "they don't live long enough to meet the good luck and good people who can help them find that other person inside them."

ten

Transcending the Past

I STARTED THIS BOOK TALKING ABOUT MY BROTHER'S DEATH. NOW my mother is dying. She's ninety-four; her time is long passed. Since she's never done anything gently or gracefully in life, her death proceeds no differently. Yet there's sadness inside me as I watch her die, sadness for what was and what wasn't between us. I haven't forgotten her cruelties or my anger. But now when I see how frail she is, how little is left of the woman who once was such a frightening and powerful presence in my life, my feelings are complicated by unaccustomed compassion.

As I reflect on our past—on who she was, on what I've become—I think about the issues of identification and *dis*identification and of the complex interweaving of the two. I remember the resolve with which I decided I would be different from her, a promise I made to myself when I was a small child and that, in important ways, I've kept. But I also know that, with all my distance, I identified sufficiently to have internalized some parts of her. So although she was the bane of my young existence, the stubborn determination that enabled her to survive a very difficult life also provided a model of the possible for me—a model that, ironically, helped me to disidentify with her and to escape the worst effects of life in my family.

I know, of course, that the child who felt the sting of my mother's angry rejection still lives inside me, even pops to the surface once in awhile and demands some attention—a reminder that the early years of life do matter. But they don't, as psychologists have insisted for so long, dictate or determine the course of a life. Instead, it's what we do with those early experiences—how we internalize them, how we define and manage them, whether we allow ourselves to be victimized by them, or whether we get up and move on each time we fall or are pushed down—that determines how we'll live our lives.

Without doubt, the particular genetic endowment we each bring into the world counts. We are not a blank slate at birth, as anyone who has ever observed two different infants can attest. But we're not bound by those constitutional givens either. Instead, they're like a template on which experience is written, like the last of a shoe on which the maker can construct an infinite variety of styles. Which means that what we learn in the world as we grow up in it can modify, even if it cannot wholly override, some of the genetic factors.

In many ways, the stories I've told here speak for themselves. The people in them haven't just managed to survive, they have transcended the worst kinds of family and social pathology—abandonment, incest, psychosis, physical and psychological brutality, alcoholism and its accompaniments. Yet they are, by any standards, living fulfilling adult lives.

Certainly, the past still lives inside them, still engages them from time to time, still catches them up in sometimes unexpected ways, still fuels some aspects of their behavior. Thus it is that Wayne Morgan traded the possibility of a woman's love for an intimate relationship with God; that Kevin McLaren still wears some of the armor he needed to protect against the violence and the psychosis in his family; that Sara Mikoulis still conjures with what she calls "the dark side" of depression from time to time; that Chris Lydon doesn't have the kind of intimate relationship with a woman he longs for; that Petar Steprovic's anger still burns hot enough to call the shots more often than is good for him.

But who among us has lived to adulthood without blemishes and imperfections, without issues that remain unresolved, problems that require our attention? For the men and women who live on these pages, the blemishes and imperfections are there, but so is their persistent refusal to give up the struggle and accept them quietly.

What's left now is to pull together some of the strands that are evident throughout these tales of triumph and to answer some questions left unsettled. I said at the beginning that marginality is the psychological bedrock on which an alternative life becomes possible. In every case, these were children who lived at the periphery of family life. Sometimes it was cruelty—physical, psychological, or both—that pushed them there; sometimes it was that they didn't fit in the family into which they were born; often it was some combination of all these things. Whatever the circumstances, their marginality made it possible to distance themselves very early in their lives, a distance that enabled them to disidentify with the family and, in doing so, to see and grasp alternatives when they came into view.

Their marginality taught them also to tolerate loneliness, to find ways to comfort themselves rather than to look to others who, they understood early on, wouldn't be there to give it. Ana Guttierez escaped into a rich fantasy life, a world where imagination took her from danger to safety, from tyranny to freedom. By the time he was four years old, Kevin McLaren was already spending a good part of his day in the basement making music on a toy piano. Lynne Halsted turned a life-size stuffed toy into a companion she could trust.

In each case there was also some kind of interest or activity—books, music, art, sports—that took them out of the family and into another world, sometimes the real one, sometimes one that lived in imagination alone. Whatever the form, each of these activities provided comfort; each was an act in the service of creating an alternative life, even if still only a fantasy; each made a difference in how they experienced the life they were living; and each displayed the kind of imaginative powers that made it possible to envision a different future.

Paradoxically, the same qualities that enabled them to ease their loneliness and comfort themselves also ensured the kind of personal attractiveness that made them what I have called *adoptable*. Their openness to experience, their willingness to join life rather than shrink from it, their gratitude for even the small kindnesses that most people take for granted, their refusal to define themselves as victims—all these drew people to them who, at various times in their lives, became the surrogates and mentors who gave them a hand up when they needed it and helped to fill gaps left by the past.

Sometimes these were long-lasting relationships. The woman who became a model and mentor for Chris Lydon was deeply involved in his life for twenty years. Sometimes they were people who passed through briefly—the landlady who, for a short time, became like a mother to Sara Mikoulis; the friend's mother who encouraged Lynne Halsted to get out of her family and into a boarding school. Sometimes they were members of a political movement—the Black Panthers who persuaded Chris Lydon that he had "the right stuff" to get through a college education.

The positive fallout from their marginality notwithstanding, it has not been without costs. In the private world, they give trust warily, tending to withdraw to safety when they feel under threat, a quality that sometimes makes for difficulty in their intimate relationships. Yet they hang in, grappling with their fears, determined not to let them run their lives. Sometimes they win the struggle; sometimes they lose. But always they keep trying.

In the public world, a lifetime of standing on the outside makes it hard to come inside, even when they've been invited to do so. It isn't simply that they don't want to. Rather, an odd combination of yearning to belong shares internal space with pride in their independence, in their outsiderness, in the belief that it gives them some special insight into the flaws and imperfections of the inside world, and perhaps most important of all, in their conviction that their creativity is linked to their marginality.

Despite their longings, therefore, they resist any invitation to move inside, certain that they can never really belong; that, no matter how hard they try, they can never fit. And they may not be wrong. A childhood in which the figures of authority are also the tormentors isn't good training for granting legitimacy to the authorities of adulthood. To live comfortably on the inside requires a willingness to yield some authority to others—a difficult feat for the men and women I've written about here who don't give themselves over easily to any authority outside themselves.

Their ambivalent and tenuous relationship with figures of authority has both positive and negative consequences in the conduct of their lives. On the negative pole, the continuing struggle against authority often leaves them feeling alienated and isolated, convinced that there's no place where they can feel both welcome and comfortable. On the positive side, it allows for a kind of independence that can foster creativity, even when they work inside bureaucratic institutions known for their rigidity and control.

Wayne Morgan, for example, is not a man who can submit comfortably to the masters of the church and their edicts. He continues to question; to search for answers that make sense to him, even when they don't accord with the canon; to develop his relationship to God in his own way without much concern for the prescribed form. Which makes him an extraordinarily humane and nonjudgmental priest, one who helps people to find their own way rather than trying to impose his. But his career has also been marked by clashes with authority that have made his life in the church far more difficult than it might otherwise have been.

In addition to their marginality, their adoptability, and their complicated relationship to authority, these men and women share a high degree of intelligence—a characteristic that not only has attracted people to them but has helped them to find creative ways to navigate their often dangerous world. By *intelligence,* I don't mean the kind that's measured with pencil-and-paper tests and results in an IQ score. I'm referring instead to the multifaceted, multilayered qualities of the mind that allow us to develop a range of competencies—the whole of which makes up what we call *intelligence* and which, because of its complexity, doesn't lend itself readily to quantification.

Intelligence, in this sense, is not some single heritable entity. Instead, as Howard Gardner, a leading developmental psychologist and student of intelligence, argues in *Frames of Mind,* intelligence comes in several forms—linguistic and logical-mathematical intelligences, musical intelligence, spatial intelligence, bodily-kinesthetic intelligence, and two forms of personal intelligence: interpersonal and *intra*personal.

Just as intelligence is not some single, measurable quality of the mind, it is also not something that inheres in the individual, something we carry around in our heads independent of the world of people and things around us. Rather, as Gardner writes, it's an interaction between an individual's potential and the opportunities and constraints that mark a particular cultural setting.

The women and men in this book exhibit a wide range of *intelligences.* Some are unique to a given person—Kevin McLaren's musical intelligence is the most obvious. Others are shared by all, most notably their linguistic intelligence, which includes the ability to develop a coherent and ego-sustaining narrative of their lives, and their interpersonal and intrapersonal intelligences, which enable them to manage both their public and private worlds successfully.

At the interpersonal level, their intelligence manifests itself in an array of qualities that may find its most vivid expression in the phrase *street smarts.* This means, among other things, that they make their way comfortably in the social world while, at the same time, they move about that world with a healthy skepticism, rarely falling victim to naive assumptions, always wary about accepting what they see around them at face value—a product, no doubt, of having grown up in an environment where the facade of family and social life was very different from the reality.

The importance of their interpersonal intelligence is matched only by the centrality of their intrapersonal intelligence in facilitating their transcendence. It's this quality that enabled them, even as young children, to understand what was going on around them and to find ways to protect against it. This is the capacity, too, that allowed for the development of an alternative sense of self—that empowered Karen Richards, for example, to fashion an identity and a definition of herself that stood in opposition to the despised image her adoptive mother held up to her.

The same intrapersonal intelligence—the ability to hold onto a self, even in the face of the assaults they suffered—made it possible to stand back and observe the fray without getting bogged down in it. They may have been pained, angered, and frightened by the events of their lives, but they retained enough distance not to get caught in endlessly blaming themselves.

Certainly, there were times when they thought they were responsible for a parent's anger, when they believed if they could only be "good enough" they could stop the misery. But they didn't get stuck there, as so many children who suffer abuse and neglect do. Instead, their distance and disidentification enabled them to construct their own narrative—a story that separated them from the pathology around them; a story that, in every case, underscored the boundary between "them" and "me."

These narratives, and the psychological separation they embody, made it possible for Lynne Halsted to suffer her mother's alcoholic beatings and say to herself, "This doesn't really have anything to do with me"; for Wayne Morgan to watch his mother sink deeper and deeper into her angry, alcoholic despair and say, "I wish I could, but I know I can't help her"; for Karen Richards to survive her mother's psychotic rages and say, "It can't be me; this woman must be crazy."

Together, their interpersonal and intrapersonal intelligence fostered the kind of intellectual and psychological restlessness that demanded that they reject easy explanations and kept them searching for their own ways of understanding. Indeed, in some ways, it was the search itself that propelled their transcendence because embedded in it was their determination not to be passive victims of their circumstances. Instead, they struggled to gain some feelings of efficacy, to maintain some sense of control, if not over external events, then over how they perceived those events and managed them internally.

It was through such striving to place what psychologists call "the locus of control" inside themselves that they took a crucial step in the development of a sense of efficacy in the world. People who consistently feel victimized by external events place the locus of control outside themselves and assure a continuing sense of victimization. But even in situations where people are regularly victimized by prejudice, discrimination, injustice, and brutality, some escape victimization, at least in part, by their conviction that they're not totally helpless—a belief that allows them to engage in a persistent struggle to retain control over some aspects of their lives, whether internal or external.

In this context, even Chris Lydon's criminal behavior can be seen as a way to take initiative in the face of the helplessness of his family and community, an attempt to gain some mastery in a world that seemed out of control. True, in his case, the alternatives available in his environment took him into a life that created a new kind of danger and the potential for self-destruction. Nevertheless, it's also true that by refusing the helpless and resigned posture so common in the community around him, he retained at least some sense of his own power to determine the course of his life, the very quality that ultimately led him to triumph over his past.

At the beginning, I wrote that "when one looks at lives in process, it seems evident that there are both continuities and discontinuities. . . ." Now at the end, it's clear that stability and continuity live alongside change and discontinuity. In some ways, the men and women on these pages are very different today than they were yesterday. "It feels like a thousand years ago, like I was somebody else then," says Chris Lydon, echoing the sentiments of the others.

In other ways, they are very much the same—in the internal qualities that enabled them to transcend their pasts, in the strategies and adaptations they used to do so. The capacity to dole out pain in doses small enough so that they aren't overwhelmed by it is as much a part of the present as it was of the past. As is their ability to retreat into a private place when the pressures of the public one become too great. The skill with which they sought and found alternative sources of support, both human and nonhuman, still makes itself felt in their adult lives. As does their ability to be involved in something larger than themselves, which, in adulthood, translates into a sense of mission, a need to feel useful, to help others who now suffer some of the hardships they know so well. The determination with which they mastered the obstacles before them in childhood is still evident in the pursuit of their goals in adulthood. As is their refusal to succumb to victimhood, no matter how difficult their lives may become.

Indeed, they abjure the culture of victimhood that's so pervasive today, seeing it as a trap that threatens to ensnare all who embrace it. "It's an alluring proposition for some people, I guess." says Petar Steprovic. "If you decide you're a victim, you can sit around feeling sorry for yourself and blaming the world for your troubles. I haven't got time for that; I've got a life to live."

It isn't that Petar and the others don't understand that they were victims of neglect, abandonment, abuse, and outright cruelty in childhood. But as important as those events were in shaping the past, they refuse to allow them to dominate the present. As Karen Richards says so pithily, "That's what *happened* to me; it's not who I *am*"—a crucial distinction, one that makes it possible to remember the past without languishing in it.

I said earlier that without memory we are adrift, unsure not just of our past but of our present, unable to trace our history, to know how we got from there to here. As Chris Lydon put it so aptly, "How do you know who you are if you just forget the past?"

For the men and women whose lives are chronicled on these pages, memory is a gift—a gift that enabled them to construct a narrative of their lives that gives form, substance, and meaning to their suffering. Each such tale is an act of creation, a blending of memory and perception that becomes its own kind of psychological truth, a story that is itself related to their transcendence. They neither deny the past nor surrender to the self-pity the culture of victimhood encourages. Instead, their memories have prodded them to action, helping them to organize their lives in the past, enabling them to understand them in the present.

The stories they tell include pain, anger, and pride—pain for their suffering, anger at the memory of the cruelties they endured, pride in their ability to fall down seven times and get up eight. Now they want to speak out, not in an act of vengeance but because in allowing their stories to be told, they affirm their history and take comfort, finally, in being heard. In finding the courage to speak publicly, they also take another step on the road to resolution, an idea given voice most clearly by Sara Mikoulis. "Your doing this book and telling my story gives me a sense of resolution I've never been able to experience before. I'm not sure why; maybe because putting it in print is like a testimony to the truth.

"Nobody ever listened to me; they never even saw me. I don't know if my mother ever knew what I really looked like. And for sure, she never had any idea who I was. Now it's like I'm standing up and saying, 'Hey, here I am, and this is what happened to me.' And seeing it in print, people will listen. It feels like it's the thing that'll finally let me put away all that ugliness from the past."

Their tales are told; the last words are spoken; the circle is closed. Sara Mikoulis, Petar Steprovic, Lynne Halsted, Wayne Morgan, Ana Guttierez, Kevin McLaren, Karen Richards, Chris Lydon—not just names on a page, but real people living real lives, daunting lives. Their stories offer testimony to the human capacity for creativity and resilience, contradicting the theories of psychological determinism that for so long have dominated our view of human development. Reading them will, I hope, empower others who are struggling to make a life in the face of adversity. For their message is clear: *We are not forever bound to be hostages to our past.*